NEW THAI STYLE

First published in 2016 by

Talisman Publishing Pte Ltd
talisman@apdsing.com
www.talismanpublishing.com

World (excluding SE Asia)
Laurence King Publishing Ltd
361-373 City Road
London EC1V 1LR, UK
Registered in England 1263586
Tel: +44 (0)20 7841 6900
Fax: +44 (0)20 7841 6910
enquiries@laurenceking.com
www.laurenceking.com
ISBN 978-178-06-7833-7

Thailand, Cambodia, Laos & Myanmar
River Books
order@riverbooksbk.com
www.riverbooksbk.com
ISBN 978-616-73-3974-0

A catalogue record for this book is available from the British Library

Art Director Norreha Sayuti
Designer Stephy Chee, Foo Chee Ying
Studio Manager Janice Ng
Copy Editor Paul Haines
Publisher Ian Pringle

Printed in Malaysia

NEW THAI STYLE

Photography **Michael Freeman**
Texts **Kim Inglis**

หัวรับน้ำดับเพลิง
SIAMESE

อดีตเคยแรง
ไม่เมา ไม่กลับ
บ้า!!แต่ว่าไม่โง่

CONTENTS

01 — 8 INTRODUCTION

02 CONTEMPORARY THAI

20 So Far, So Good
26 A Collector's Vista
32 Wood and White
38 Hospitality Hub
44 A Carefully Curated Home
50 Where Architecture meets Nature
56 A Calm Serenity
60 Urban Courtyard Home

03 THAI ESCAPES

68 An Airy Eyrie
76 A Taste of Old Siam
84 Contemporary meets Colonial
88 On the Veranda
94 A Haven of Calm
102 A Treasury for Book-Lovers
108 A Hillside Hideaway
112 A Real Treasure

04 LIVING WITH NATURE

118 Among the Rocks of Santikhiri
126 Spa in the Forest
132 A Penthouse in Bangkok
138 Urban Tree House
144 Baan Suan Sanghob

05 HERITAGE THAI

152 Tassana Pra
158 Baan Khampun
164 Baan Mier Raap
170 Thai Art in a Modern Home
176 Reworking Tradition
180 Chakrabongse House and Villas
188 Riverside Retreat

192 ACKNOWLEDGEMENTS/ LISTINGS/CREDITS

INTRODUCTION

The concept of "Thai Style", adopted a couple of decades ago and exported around the globe, has now become a household term. People all over the world see a soaring Thai roof, a meticulously lacquered ceremonial container or a stucco temple motif and immediately label it as Thai. The graceful form, the flamboyant flourish of the craftsman's design, the mix of the spiritual, the natural and the supernatural are all features of a Thai-style building, artefact or piece of art. Somehow this combination of elements jumps out at the viewer as unmistakably Thai.

What is not so well known is how these approaches have been updated in the last decade or so to produce a thoroughly contemporary Thai Style — one that merges ancient practices with modern fashions, graphics and technologies. The skills honed over the centuries by latter-day craftsmen have been taken to the next stage by innovative architects, designers, furniture and product designers, and more. We showcase their work in this book.

Time-honoured Thai Style is especially evident in historical buildings: An elegant Ayutthaya-style wooden house on stilts or the tapering shape of a northern Thai temple is now embedded in our consciousness as Thai Style. The way buildings communicate with and are assimilated into their surrounding nature is another classic feature of Thai architecture — the spaces outside are as important, or as integral, as those within. In the contemporary context, it may be slightly more difficult to categorise obviously Thai elements. Some architects talk here of the Thai experience, rather than Thai motifs, styles and forms — and this is a concept we look closely at in the ensuing pages.

The same can be said for interior design, art and crafts. There are obvious Thai-style schools of painting, the craft of casting in bronze images of the Buddha, the designs of various furniture pieces painstakingly carved for temple and palace, as well as other smaller items made from wood, lacquer and ceramic. Thais have an innate sense of beauty and are able to imbue their arts and crafts with refinement; they are also good at modifying other people's designs and making them innately Thai. In the home, Thai items mix seamlessly with Western elements. This is somehow surprising

when one considers the current global tendency towards clarity and simplicity in interior design.

It is the intention of this book to showcase how Thai Style has evolved over the past couple of decades. A number of different homes, resorts, hotels and residences have been selected from all over the country; for the most part, they are reasonably new. Some are built to mimic old styles, some are re-builds and some are completely new. Most are designed by established and emerging architects and designers, while some are built to the specifications of a particular visionary. Each has been selected to showcase a newer confident aesthetic that has emerged in recent years — one that breaks new ground but nevertheless remains distinctly Thai.

Architecture in Thailand

Historically, the story of architecture in Thailand has been one of cultural adoption and assimilation. As populations have moved and settled within the Siam area, they have brought with them influences from outside. Shapes, lines and motifs from India, Sri Lanka, the Mon people, Burma, Laos, China and even classical Europe can be seen in many different permutations in traditional Thai buildings. Hybrid form is the norm.

One of the most visited buildings in Thailand showcases this amalgamation of forms perfectly — the throne hall at the Chakri Maha Prasat in the Grand Palace in Bangkok. Designed in 1876 and built by King Chulalongkorn (Rama V), it juxtaposes a cascading series of multi-tiered roofs atop a foundation that is 100 percent Baroque in style. Used for receptions, state banquets and other ceremonial purposes, its interiors are similarly hybridized. Eastern- and Western-inspired opulence vie for attention in a glittering haze of red and gold. Similarly, many famous temples in the north of Thailand incorporate Lao and even Chinese architectural principles in their design and form, while Sukhothai temples incorporate designs borrowed from Khmer and Indian sources.

PREVIOUS PAGE / A green and airy courtyard in the principal building at Bangkok's swish Siam Hotel.

OPPOSITE / Showcasing the beauty of rattan, an elegant outdoor lounger with tapering tip sits in the courtyard of a restaurant on the Ping River outside Chiang Mai. A simple *sala* with characteristic curved roof acts as the boat landing jetty.

ABOVE / Three traditional Thai rooms showcase the timeless beauty of teak. Left to right: a carved and gilded scripture cabinet sits between intricately patterned red-and-gold pillars at Wat Rakang in Bangkok; a *howdah* seat and intricately carved day bed offer scant furnishing in a capacious upper hall at Ban Wongburi in Phrae; the hall of Bangkok's Plainoen Mansion, built for Prince Naris, houses a beautiful collection of Ayutthaya-period lacquer chests used for storing clothes and books.

Arguably, however, it is in domestic architecture that one finds the strongest exemplification of Thai Style — and, more specifically, in the form of the classic central plains wooden house on stilts. Instantly recognizable, such a house has distinctive curved roof ends or bargeboards, inward-sloping teak-panelled walls and a large raised verandah that connects the separate rooms. The open space beneath the house serves a number of practical functions from animal husbandry to providing respite from seasonal flooding, while the whole is transportable and extendable. All parts of the home may be dismantled, moved to a new site and reassembled, and it is easy for other rooms and structures to be added.

Eminently pragmatic, such homes are found all over the country. Because teak is highly durable and the style has garnered legions of fans, such homes continue to be built today. Parts of — or even entire homes — are assembled from old edifices; sometimes the columns may be old while other parts are new. Suited to both climate and culture, these houses hold a special place in the hearts of Thais and foreign residents alike.

In this book we feature a couple of such houses, along with a number of structures built or re-built in the Lanna style of the north, incorporating Chinese, Khmer and Lao influences, as well as some hotels and residences that take the beauty of Thailand's stunning scenery as their inspiration. Typically, Thais lived outdoors, with most social activities taking place on the huge raised *chan-ban* verandah that connected the various rooms of the domestic house. Due to issues surrounding sustainability as well as a desire to incorporate nature into contemporary living, many architects have included the outdoors, in one form or another, in their designs. Similarly, landscaping has improved phenomenally, whilst respect for the surrounding land and spirits of the land is, for the most part, maintained.

Of course, Thailand was never colonized, but there are many examples of a colonial style in Thailand. The teak trade in the north was largely managed by expatriates, and, naturally, there were foreign legations and residences from the mid 19th century onwards in Bangkok. The Anglo-Indian bungalow prototype, ubiquitous wherever the English settled in

ABOVE AND OPPOSITE / Water and the open air are key features in the tropical Thai home, be it a modern residence or traditional wooden house on stilts. Left to right: a rooftop pool with water plants enlivens and cools a penthouse deck; cross ventilation in the form of huge French doors and windows cools the first-floor living room in an Ayutthaya-style house; a sleek inifinity pool fronts a modern home in Koh Samui; colonial-style seating nook on a cool verandah at the Ping Nakara Boutique Hotel in Chiang Mai; picture window view of the sea from a bathroom in the modern Serenity House in Phuket designed by Duangrit Bunnag.

Asia, is found in many parts of Thailand because of its sensible approach to the tropical climate. These factors, as well as the Thai ability to assimilate the best from the West, have resulted in buildings that incorporate colonial aspects in their design. Similarly, as Thailand has modernized, the old has given way to the new. High-rise apartment blocks replace walk-ups — but it is encouraging to note that many retain some semblance of Thai style in their interiors.

At first glance, many modern houses, especially those in urban areas and popular holiday resorts, seem rooted in a milieu much more Western than Thai. Modern materials such as concrete, glass and steel, architectural forms including flat roofs and open-plan rooms, and an aesthetic that borrows more from mid-century modern designers and architects than Asian culture, do not appear remotely "Thai". However, careful consideration of such villas and homes reveals seemingly hidden cultural elements. Sometimes these come in the form of the arrangement of spaces, in the way a building interacts with its environment (land, water, sea, horizon), or through subtle detailing. Often, however, its "Thai-ness" is embedded in the "Thai experience" of living in the house — how a relaxed Thai lifestyle, incorporating as it does *subai-subai* (chilling out) with *sanuk* (fun), fits perfectly with the architecture.

Thailand, today, is a bewildering mix of the contemporary and the traditional. Thrusting skyscrapers sit side by side with ornately decorated temple complexes; Chinese shophouses, colonial-style residences, bland concrete bungalows and exuberant palaces vie for attention on crowded city streets. Many of the old *klongs* or canals have been converted into roads, but waterways still play a vital role in the country. Especially in Bangkok, the old is replaced by the new with startling speed. A recent visit to the once sleepy seaside town of Hua Hin — now transformed into a chaotic market town — illustrates how great is the pace of change.

Nonetheless, amidst the urban sprawl and the rush for "development", there is plenty that is new, yet traditional. Many contemporary architects are still responding to climate, landscape and community in a sensitive fashion, but combining

ABOVE / The Thai love of decorative objects and the importance of finely wrought craftsmanship is evident in these treasures. Clockwise from top left: a tea set with beautiful green tree pattern and a blue-and-white ceramic teapot at Ban Mor Lek, Bangkok; assorted treasures from the Silver House on Ramkanheang Road collected by Dr Manas Soongprasit who has a passion for Thai royal art and *objets d'art*: silver tea and coffee sets, with Thai patterning but Western in style, reign of Rama VIII–IX; Western-style salt and pepper shakers, same era; silver trays with figurines derived from *khon* performances used for flower offerings, reign of King Rama V; a table setting fit for a King includes a silver nielloware platter which once belonged to King Rama VIII with his initials on the platter, along with some sweet wash basins with *hongse* decoration and assorted glassware.

this aesthetic with new building materials, styles and technologies. As architect, Duangrit Bunnag, notes: "Every Thai architect has Thai designs embedded in their subconscious. No matter the language of architecture we use, we always deliver a hidden agenda in terms of living in a Thai way."

Thai Design and Craftsmanship

Two fundamental tenets of the Thai DNA are the Buddhist faith and the people's veneration of the monarchy. As such, they are key in any understanding of Thai arts and crafts.

In the past, most design centred around the *wat* (temple) and the palace. Over the centuries countless buildings to venerate the Buddha and the King were built — and during this time a rich tradition of craftsmanship flourished. Craftsmen took influences from both without and within the country and created a huge number of items (both secular and religious) that can instantly be identifiable as Thai. Be they Buddha images or temple accoutrements, such as manuscript cabinets, altars, ceremonial containers and so on, personal objects, royal regalia, or items for the home such as ceramics, textiles and more, they share a rich tradition of design and craftsmanship.

Many items — a lacquered cabinet, a ceramic jar or a betel-nut box inlaid with mother-of-pearl — have a unique Thai identity. In large part, this is because of the shape, decoration (often using intricate floral and vegetal motifs), inherent artistry and form. What's interesting is how such items have evolved, where their influences came from, and how they are being adapted and modified for the future.

Decorative arts in the form of lacquerware, woodcarving, stuccowork, glass mosaics, ceramics and textiles are some of the more traditional art forms in Thailand. Recurring motifs, an exuberant use of colour, a sense of humour and elegant proportions are seen again and again. Development and refinement also occurred in the manufacture of ceramics and

elegant wares often produced under royal patronage. King Rama V was instrumental in bringing Western culture in the form of architecture, habits and clothing into Thai life. As a result, a whole industry of Western utensils decorated with Thai motifs and patterns emerged (see opposite).

In some of the homes and hotels featured in this book we get a chance to view some fine collections of such *objets d'art*. In the context of today's world, it is encouraging to see how such items, along with more utilitarian wares (baskets, rugs, textiles) are used in domestic interiors.

Mixing the antique with the contemporary can be a tricky business, but somehow Thai accents and artefacts fit very well in the contemporary home. A collection of lacquered monk's alms bowls lined on a shelf, a carving from a temple above a bed, or even one single Thai-style adornment can transform an interior. And because the arts are encouraged and emulated in Thailand, they continue to develop: a heavily carved altar table inspires a streamlined console; a carved doorframe is used as a headboard; a *hsun-ok* is recreated in startling white ceramic (see page 1). Artists and artisans are once again taking influences from the outside world to produce new and unusual designs.

Whilst imagination has never been in short supply, quality has been an issue in the past. Thankfully the advent of new mechanization, materials and facilities has resulted in an improvement in this sector. Standards, especially in the finishing, are now export-quality — and Thai goods are in demand across the globe.

Contemporary Interior Design

Traditionally, Thai homes didn't contain much in the way of furniture with the exception of mats for sleeping and the odd low-level platform or *tang* with Chinese-style legs. Decoration was either carved into the fabric of the home or was reserved for the temple and/or palace. Daily activities took place on the floor which was kept meticulously clean.

ABOVE / Modern homes in Thailand are no less inventive when it comes to decorative items. Left to right: a black lacquer console displays a medley of carved panels with gold leaf and inlaid glass. Taken from a Burmese temple, they are mounted on bronze stands; the old and the new, the sacred and the profane — a pairing that defies convention; mother-of pearl wares inlaid into red lacquer are the result of hours of labour; tiny pieces of the nacreous inner layer of molluscs are mounted onto lacquered wares, after multiple filings reveal their colour and shine.

As time passed, Western attitudes and practices permeated the country and with them came the concept of furniture, furnishings, interior décor and less traditional lifestyles. Even in the mid 19th century, Siam was forward-looking enough to take Western knowledge and use it for its own ends.

In the beginning, such knowledge was reserved for royalty and those at court, but as the country developed, it began to be embraced by all strata of society. Later, the royal and the religious were able to enter the realm of the ordinary populace.

This can be seen in many a home, hotel and resort today. Specialist workmanship, such as gold-leaf stenciling and silk weaving, has transferred from the *wat* to the wellbeing centre, from the temple to the tavern. Palace wares are bought at auction and displayed in ordinary people's homes, while items like highly polished lacquerwares and the finest silks and celadons are routinely used in living rooms and bedrooms as decoration and homewares. Many homes have a scripture cabinet doubling up as a television console, or a temple gable acting as an artwork.

In a reversal of fortune, some of the rustic wares and rural practices in the domain of farming communities have found new life in the urban environment. Organizations such as the Queen Sirikit Support Foundation and a variety of NGOs have encouraged mainly tribal artisans to adapt their traditions to supply and facilitate modern-day "progress". Basket makers, woodcarvers, weavers, ceramicists and the like are utilizing their Thai-and-tested skills into crafting accessories for the high-end home. The range of furniture, vases, mats, trays, cushion covers and runners, to mention only a few products on the market both within Thailand and made for export, is now enormous. What was once a utilitarian tradition has become a global behemoth.

Entertaining, decorating, flower-arranging, and such like with a Thai twist are all bona fide businesses in their own right these days. There are schools that teach people culinary and table-arranging skills; artisan centres that produce homewares from gold- and silverware to celadon; product designers that adapt traditional nielloware and *bencharong*

styles into contemporary tablewares; and interior designers that are adept at matching the antique with the avant-garde. As long as there is some association with Thai styles, motifs (the Thai elephant has proved popular), materials and more, there seems to be no stopping this trend.

As with architecture, interior design is also about experiencing Thai culture. A few of the hotels we feature within these pages seek to celebrate both past and present by allowing guests to immerse themselves in a country that is known for magic and mysticism, as well as its free spirit and fun-loving nature. Whether they celebrate Thai practices such as massage and Muay Thai boxing, the traditional steam chamber with exotic herbs, or the myriad tastes and smells of the Thai kitchen and garden is immaterial. They do it in a way that appeals to contemporary tastes: meditation in the hills of Koh Samui; contemplation in the northern hill country; cooking classes on the Chao Phraya river are all conducted in sybaritic surrounds.

Conclusion

As Thais have appropriated outside influences in the past, outsiders flock to Thailand to partake of Thai lifestyles today. Foreign residents account for more than a handful of the home-owners in this book, and the featured hotels, hostels, resorts and spas are well patronized by overseas and local tourists alike. An edgy, graphic-filled backpackers' haunt, a luxury five-star oasis and an eco-friendly urban hideaway are only a few types of destination we showcase. There are also some inspired "escapes" — retreats where visitors can shed the stresses of modern-day life — as well as some hip and happening metropolitan inns.

Through the centuries, Thailand has been a place where visitors have naturally felt at ease — and this has led to people returning again and again. Luckily, Thais are inventive and imaginative enough to keep developing their offering. We hope this book whets the appetite for more.

OPPOSITE AND ABOVE / Many modern homes in Thailand are notable for their inventive pairing of Thai, Chinese and Western furniture and furnishings with decorative items from all over Asia. Left to right: a *chofa* or roof finial probably removed from a monastery and mounted on a stand is in the form of a mythical swan or *hongse*. It takes pride of place on the desk of Cindi Novkov's home in Chiang Mai; Chinese scholars' chairs flank an altar table in a home in Bangkok; a fine Indian wooden door is used as a decorative piece at the end of an apartment corridor; a Chinese day bed with fine gilt carving is decorated with Thai silk in rich red tones; a pristine bedroom at Bangkok's Sofitel So hotel features sleek metallic details designed by Somchai Jongsaeng of Deca Atelier.

OVERLEAF / A serene inner courtyard at the Rachamankha hotel in Chiang Mai celebrates local Lanna heritage and provides a peaceful retreat for travellers.

CONTEMPORARY THAI

Thai Style has always been permeable to outside influences, and it may be this combination of time-honoured traditions and new styles, materials and methods of craftsmanship that makes contemporary Thai design so attractive. Mixing old and new, Western and Oriental, and the natural with the artificial produces marvellous results in the ateliers of Thai artisans.

Put an innately talented and enquiring collection of craftsmen, architects, designers and the like with a plethora of wonderful materials (lacquer, wood, silks, to name a few) and a centuries-old tradition of arts and crafts — and we end up with some truly special interiors. Sometimes, the results look minimalist and pared-down; at others they are flamboyant and fun. Either way, they are imbued with a uniquely graceful ethos that is entirely Thai.

ABOVE / Minute pieces of mother-of-pearl and shell glow with luminosity on a contemporary décor item.

OPPOSITE / Close-up of bamboo, string and artisanal paper covering the pendant lamps at Bangkok's chic Sofitel So hotel.

So Far, So Good

As is the trend with hotel chains, Sofitel launched a new brand in 2011, one that is design-conscious, urbane and aimed at travellers who are looking for more style and personality in their accommodations. So far, Sofitel So hotels have opened in Mauritius, Singapore and Bangkok: each utilises a high-end design "name", usually French as Sofitel is a French brand, who works in combination with a local creative team. So far, so good, as they say at Sofitel So. The results have been promising.

Kenzo Tadaka, the noted Japanese fashion designer worked magic in Mauritius, while no lesser worthy than Karl Lagerfeld devised a Lion's Seal motif for the Lion City of Singapore's Sofitel So. In Bangkok, celebrated French fashion designer Christian Lacroix lent a Baroque touch to its high-rise hotel, working with award-winning architect Smith Obayawat and five famous Thai interior designers. The outcome of this fruitful collaboration is a thoroughly modern, material structure that nevertheless takes the five elements — water, earth, wood, metal and fire — into its interior design ethos.

RIGHT / Situated on the 29th floor with views over Lumpini Park, HI-SO bar and restaurant is particularly magical at night.

THIS PAGE AND OPPOSITE TOP / Nithi Sthapitanonda, Thai national artist and founder of 49 Group, designed the Wood element spaces where wood and light interact to sensational effect.

OPPOSITE BELOW / Nauralistic, yet sumptuous, décor in the spa suites was inspired by the mythological Himmapan Forest of Thai tradition.

Behind the high-tech façade of this curvy, metallic-shaded high-rise resting on a glass, zinc and stone podium is a striking interior — at once eye-catching and playful. Public spaces are characterized by the fire element — most emphatically this is realized in the signature Red Oven restaurant — yet other spaces have a warmth and wit that is doubtless energizing. The other four elements are reserved for the 238 guest rooms and suites: a dark and mysterious water scheme; a grounded earth theme with ravishing blue primeval wall paintings; a calming wood palate for tranquility; and sleek white and bright spaces with metallic details in the last category. Naturally, guests can request their accommodation of choice in advance.

Since it has opened the Sofitel So has become a bit of a hub with local creatives and has been no less successful with those from out of town. With an enviable location overlooking Lumpini Park, the hotel rooftop has become a popular meeting place. Both the swimming pool with its series of elegant cabanas and the Park Society restaurant and bar are trendy venues for young urbanites. There is a high-tech element in the hotel's facilities and a natural ambiance in both interiors and views.

We will leave the last word to Robert Gaymer-Jones, Sofitel's CEO: "The name 'So', derived from Sofitel, is also meant to emphasize a great degree as in 'so hip' or 'so cool'," he notes, "and this brand is certainly a contemporary lifestyle brand that is geared towards the fashion-conscious guest." So there.

LEFT TOP / An outdoor terrace at the Red Oven restaurant, designed by London's Gorgeous Group, features a wall-sized cartological representation of Bangkok, a marble bar (just seen on right) and casual seating.

LEFT BOTTOM AND OPPOSITE FAR RIGHT / Sleek metallic details from the Metal rooms were designed by Somchai Jongsaeng of Deca Atelier. These bedrooms are for purists, pairing stark white modernist walls and linens with silver metallic trimmings.

OPPOSITE / Three views of the Earth element rooms, designed by Vitoon Kunalungkarn of IAW Design, showcase a ravishing deep blue and white colour scheme. The graphics are inspired by primeval wall paintings from Thailand, while the linens are whiter than white.

A Collector's Vista

Built high in the hills of Koh Samui above the beaches of Chaweng Yai and Chaweng Noi, with views to Bophut and beyond to the neighbouring island of Koh Phangan, this elegant home is the work of owner Mom Rajawongse Charuvan Rangsit. A painter and collector, she conceptualized both house and interiors and used local architects and engineers to finalize her technical drawings. She had long dreamed of putting all her precious

collection of *objets d'art*, furniture, paintings and artifacts in one place. The result is a labour of love.

Built from local stone, with white sandstone for terraces and steps and roughly hewn local grey stone as cladding, the home is built on a steep slope. It seems to cascade down the hillside, in a series of jagged terraces. The ground floor with service area consists of a two-bedroom apartment with a private pool; above are two suites separated by a central dip pool; the top level is the two-storey main house with terrace, pool and two guest villas, one on each side of the central structure. Charuvan Rangsit describes her home as "colonial style with sandstone columns and structures, exotic living with Moroccan furniture — silk embroidered poufs and fabulous lamps from Marrakesh; antiques and paintings from my collection; and, most importantly, I'm very fond of my antique doors from Pakistan and and Indonesia I have been collecting for 30 years."

ABOVE / The home is both palatial and intimate. Built on a plot of one and a half *rai* (over 2,500 square metres), the materials are all high quality: sandstone, locally hewn rock, marble and teakwood.

As the views are all encompassing, one may be tempted to sit out by the pool drinking in vistas of sea and horizon, but the interiors are well worth exploring too. There's a cozy Moroccan-style library, a capacious living room with an assortment of collectibles, some wonderfully appointed bedrooms and a beautiful verandah for dining. Most walls are painted with a special textured paint that gives an antique feeling, while the floors are cool underfoot in dark polished wood. Bathrooms are no less opulent: finished with polished sandstone, they house enormous tubs in terrazzo.

One of the highlights of the home is its access. Leaving one's vehicle at a lower parking area, one walks up a flight of 41 steps cut between giant boulders and jungle-like plantings up to a pair of intricately carved antique Pakistani doors. From here, one enters the luxurious living room that opens to a covered verandah with serene pool and sensuously slung *sala* alongside. Beyond is the infinite horizon. If it is nighttime, candles from Moroccan lanterns illuminate the surrounds, while sea and sky merge in a dramatic deep blue. Lights from boats and Koh Phangan flicker in the distance — and an atmosphere of sweet serenity prevails.

ABOVE / The main living room is a repository for many of Charuvan Rangsit's treasures: In foreground on a typical coffeeshop marble table is an exquisite lacquerware container from Burma. The antique Chinese console on left, flanked by two huge jars from Marrakesh, houses a collection of Burmese Buddha images. Above is a painting of Borobudur by John Van Der Sterren, a Dutch painter who lives in Java. The extravagantly carved door at the far end is the main door to the home.

OPPOSITE / Exterior balconies, decks and verandahs feature a mix of all-weather mock rattan furniture with antique teakwood benches and metal and glass outdoor lighting.

LEFT / One of the guest bedrooms features bed linen fabricated from a bright red hill tribe weave.

RIGHT TOP / The master bedroom is an extravagant Oriental retreat in tones of rust and ochre. The bed was custom-crafted in Chiang Mai and utilizes a set of old Chinese windows as its headboard. The screeen behind, fashioned from six antique Chinese doors, conceals the entrance to the bathroom and dressing room. An adjacent office area comprises a Chinese scholar's style red lacquered desk and chair in front of a Chinese wedding cabinet. Wide French doors lead out to a terrace that affords the best views of Koh Phangan.

RIGHT / A large picture window adjacent to the terrazzo tub in the master bath-room overlooks the garden; it is especially evocative at night when the huge rock is illuminated by a spotlight.

Wood and White

Both a refuge and an inspiration to owner Michelle Han, this wood-and-white penthouse apartment is a marvellous East meets West combo. Set on the 11th floor of a swanky apartment block in Bangkok's central business district, it's a bolthole for Han when she visits the capital.

Even though the layout is unmistakably Western, many of Han's precious possessions are Asian — Thai, Burmese, Indonesian, to name a few — and the whole apartment has a subtle Oriental feel. Nonetheless, it is thoroughly contemporary, even a little minimalist, with all the conveniences of modern life.

ABOVE / The spacious outdoor terrace is a rarity in Bangkok. Thoroughly modern in style, it features in-built seating, a polished concrete and pebble floor and strictly regimented stands of bulrushes.

LEFT / Terrace cushions are covered in a beige-and-pink fabric bearing Han's favourite batik pattern, the famous cloud motif from Cirebon. Batik patterns that originated in Cirebon on the Java Sea were influenced by Chinese, Arab and Indian traders. This one is called *mega mendung* that translates as "big cloud" motif. Taken directly from ancient Chinese iconography, the clouds infer rain, with a symbolic significance of fertility and life.

BELOW LEFT / A resin sculpture in the shape of a continuous fish ring sits on a console in the living room. Han believes it is of Chinese origin, an infinity symbol of heaven, abundance and longevity. The fish eyes are inset with luminous mother-of-pearl.

BELOW RIGHT / A rare splash of colour is achieved through this bright scarlet heliconia arrangement in a backlit display niche in the dining room.

OPPOSITE / A corner of the spacious living room features a comfy yet elegant chair and footstool, the design of which is an adaptation of one of the rattan furniture lines developed by the McGuire company in San Francisco. The low table with ginger arrangement is a hand-beaten iron stool sourced in Bangkok. Just seen on right is an oversized mirror set in an antique Indian doorframe.

One of the main attractions is the large outdoor terrace that was designed as an extension of the living room by Victor Choong, a Bangkok-based landscaper. Han wanted something that was low maintenance but comfortable, so Choong obliged by incorporating a cosy lounging platform at one end. Made from artificial wood (thereby termite resistant) with faux leather cushions that are waterproof, there's no need to remove the seating during Bangkok's frequent tropical showers. With a low *khantoke* table and slouchy cushions, it is perfect for outdoor relaxation.

The rest of the terrace is minimal, but thoroughly attractive. The perimeter is lined with custom-crafted resin planters housing a row of bulrushes set in water and the floor is a sophisticated combination of polished concrete inset with grey pebbles. A concrete container planted with one large pandanus breaks the uniform line to arrest the eye. A typical marble-topped *kopitiam* table with stools purchased from an antique shop in Chiang Mai is useful for al fresco eating, while subtle concealed outdoor lighting illuminates the scene.

ABOVE / A monochrome palette in the guest bedroom keeps things serene, as does the Chinese embroidered bed linen in pristine white. A backlit built-in shelving unit runs behind the beds and wraps around at the corner into a desk. The calligraphy print is by Irene Chou, a Chinese artist who was one of the most influential exponents of the New Ink Painting school. The photograph above the desk, depicting a detail of girls' elaborate hair ornaments touched with ink paint, is by Bali-based international photographer Rio Helmi. The Balinese theme continues with a collection of beaten silver offering boxes.

OPPOSITE TOP / In Chiang Mai, Lanna-Thai Antiques, a treasure trove of Thai and Burmese ceramics, tiles, carved panels, teak furniture, marble figurines, lacquerware and decorative items is a favourite of apartment owner, Michelle Han. These beautiful lacquerware containers were sourced there a few years ago and kept in storage until this space in the study area became available. On left, a pair of Chinese screen doors are partially visible.

OPPOSITE BOTTOM / A sturdy antique Indian door with brass knockers is used as a decorative motif in this corridor.

The interiors are no less refined, with an open-plan living and dining room cum kitchen that sports a neutral palette enlivened with dark wood, and a couple of restful bedrooms. At one end of the living room, partially segregated from the room proper by a partition of Chinese screen doors, is a practical and beautiful study area. A work desk sits in front of a dark wood shelving unit lined with monks' alms containers in red and black lacquer sourced from a handicraft shop in Chiang Mai.

Han has cleverly enlarged the room using an antique doorframe inset with a mirror at one end, while the door itself is hung as a decorative piece elsewhere in the home. It's touches like these that elevate the apartment and create élan. Cool and classy within and without, the outdoor terrace is ever present — and the inside no less tropical with large flower arrangements of ginger, heliconia and orchids.

Hospitality Hub

Young travellers who are looking for affordable accommodation in Bangkok, but are also mindful of Thai ambiance, atmosphere and design, would be hard pushed to find somewhere with more style than the lub.D hostel. Part of the Narai hotel chain, its on-trend look was developed by designLAB, a studio whose work includes museum and exhibition designs, as well as retail, hospitality and industrial projects.

The site originally housed an old warehouse, but rather than try for a re-fit DesignLAB tore it down and replaced it with two concrete blocks, one of which has a bright green painted face. The lobby with an Internet area, recreation space, reading room and bar is welcoming and unthreatening — it acts as a space for travellers of all cultures to congregate. Painted with a number of different constellations, it seems to indicate that whatever your nationality, culture or beliefs, we all live under the same sky.

Accommodations are in the two four-storey blocks and are separated by a communal courtyard. Wherever you look there are bright, primary colours, clever graphics, various images of destinations, maps and tourist sites — all underpinning the idea of a journey through Bangkok. Various chill or breakout areas encourage interaction between guests, while a variety of rooms — from dormitories, to twins, to doubles — are characterized by vibrant coloured silk-screens and clever space-planning. Whether it is an economy, standard or more luxurious room doesn't matter: The lack of space is more than compensated for by thoughtful additions in the form of a reading light, shelf, power socket, locker and privacy curtain.

The courtyard serves a double function — it allows sunlight to enter by day but also has chairs and tables for guest encounters and utilities such as washing and drying machines. Both utilitarian and sociable, it appears to mimic the overall ethos behind the hostel.

In many ways lub.D is representative of a new generation of young Thai designers: the company is savvy, smart, design-conscious, but doesn't take itself too seriously. A similar feel is found amongst other young creatives, such as furniture and product designers whose funky wares are increasingly being recognized globally. They seem to be saying that the end results must be utilitarian, the function needs to work as well as the form, but it's fun to create an amusing experience whilst you go about it.

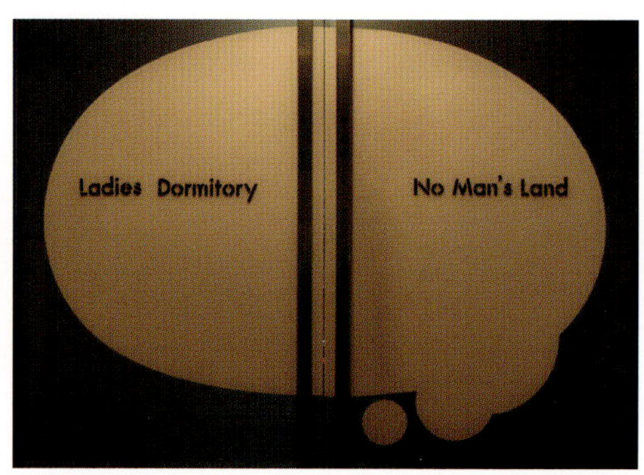

LEFT / Nopadol Limwatanakul of designLAB was also responsible for the company's first hostel in Siam Square. There, as here, architecture is minimal, but the use of graphics lifts the end product.

RIGHT / An indoor courtyard extends up to the height of the fourth floor and separates the rooms on both sides of the bulding. It invites in natural light and air during the day, and acts as a communal space for guests.

TAXI

LEFT / Whimsical touches in the décor include the placing of a brightly painted Thai *tuk tuk* as extra seating in the lobby. *Tuk tuks* are a beloved mode of transport in the city.

ABOVE / In keeping with the fun vibe, this poster for a travellers's party is in bright orange on a black background.

OVERLEAF / Public and private areas are linked by matching colour schemes, while funky imagery of destinations and journeys is silkscreened directly onto the walls of the guest rooms.

The place where towering
bargains are to be found

Hey, if you get bitten
you're in good hands
Cave - dwelling
SNAKE FARM
Venomous snake
Nocturnal
species
Lub.d
Rama 1 Rd.
Rama 4 Rd.

A Carefully Curated Home

Having lived in Asia for over 40 years, Patricia and Richard Frost have amassed an impressive collection of predominantly Thai, Chinese and Burmese antiques, all of which are displayed with flair in this spacious apartment. Set on the banks of the Chao Phraya river in an old block between the Shangri-La and Mandarin Oriental hotels, the home is located on the seventh floor.

Patricia was born in Thailand and has lived most of her adult life in Malaysia, Singapore, Hong Kong and Thailand and has travelled extensively in the region. An interior designer, she is well known both locally and internationally for her deep knowledge of Asian art, design trends and interior furnishings; she also has great connections and a real skill in sourcing. A stickler for quality, Patricia's work is defined by a cosmopolitan refinement, yet there is usually a taste of the Orient in the mix as well.

For her own home, Patricia carefully curates loved artefacts in groups that best showcase their finer qualities. She is especially keen on *zitan* and *huanghuali*, two woods that have historically been valued in China especially during the Ming and Qing Dynasty periods, and showcases a couple of prime pieces from the former. In fact, the sober aesthetic of the Ming is apparent throughout.

Dark wooden furniture and a superb polished timber floor, along with cream walls and a comfortable, homely feel, characterize the ambience of the large, airy living and dining space. Cool cream upholstered sofas with a matching cream rug are the neutral pieces, while colour and panache are added through an antique Art Deco Chinese *khotan* rug, a couple of key artworks, and hand-painted silk scatter cushions. Of particular note is an antique teakwood cabinet from Thailand with a beautiful silver collection of Thai, Burmese and Cambodian betel boxes, betel leaf holders and offering bowls, some Western-style Chinese export silver as well as an antique ceramic peach fruit collection.

As befits one of the older apartment blocks in Bangkok, there is a sizeable balcony with views over the river. Here, there is plenty of room for outdoor relaxation on a low-level *tang*/sofa with triangular cushions, or at a coffee-shop-style round marble-topped table with bentwood chairs. On cooler days, this area serves as the perfect foil to the fully air-conditioned interior.

OPPOSITE, FROM LEFT TO RIGHT / A lovely Thai candle, a Burmese papier-maché Buddha head, and a Burmese bronze offering tray. The strong ochre colours of the marigold garland are reminiscent of the robes worn by Thai and Burmese monks. A pair of beautiful antique gold and black lacquer boxes from Burma. Detail of a carved panel with gold leaf and inlaid glass from a Burmese temple, now mounted as a sculpture. Silver within a carved teak cabinet.

ABOVE / The open-plan living room is handsome yet homely. Two antique *zitan* chairs with hand-painted Chinese silk cushions face a coffee table fashioned from a chest. In front of this is a fine bamboo and carved wood Chinese double pillow. Displayed on the table are a collection of loved artefacts: carved coconut shells with sterling silver detailed rims from Thailand; a Chinese oxblood ceramic bowl on a rosewood stand; some carved jade beads and curios in a wooden offering bowl; some carved jade stands. An antique embroidered shawl from Hungary that used to belong to Patricia's great grandmother is encased in acrylic and hangs on the wall behind the sofa. The sofas are flanked by two black lacquer tables that were purchased in Hong Kong, while the aquamarine Chinese-style stool is from one of the ceramic ateliers in Ratchaburi.

ABOVE / A corner niche is dominated by an old painting depicting junks in the South China Seas at sunset; the artist is Filipino, but otherwise unknown, a mystery that intrigues its owners who want to find out more of its provenance. In the corner is a Classical tapered round-cornered elmwood cabinet set at an angle, atop of which are some antique Burmese lacquer baskets. A pair of *zitan* tea tables display some burl, *huanghuali* and *zitan* paint brush pots, collected during the owners' travels. At left is the dining area.

OPPOSITE / Coconut wood, *zitan*, an antique textile, silk and silver: the Frosts are happy to mix provenance and products that remind them of past journeys and happy holidays.

龍

ABOVE / Outside on the terrace attention to detail is illustrated by the artefacts: a couple of bronze lily pods that double up as tealight candle holders; a Shiwan jade green glazed ceramic teapot and an Asian game. The Frosts are not sure, but think the game is a form of local chess.

OPPOSITE / Cream, white and wood characterize the design palette in the bathrooms. A Chinese-style stool sports a cracked eggshell glaze, while a bamboo ladder doubles up as an elegant towel rail.

Where Architecture meets Nature

Duangrit Bunnag, an architect renowned both within Thailand and overseas, utilises a modern architectural vocabulary in his house and resort designs, but nonetheless is informed by tradition, culture and history. If the project is in Thailand, as is this estate on secluded Natai Beach in Phang Nga, he takes into consideration Thai architectural principles in both planning and execution.

Five glassed pavilions, constructed from steel and concrete, with masonry, laminate wood, teak, granite, marble and exposed brick finishings, certainly do not look "Thai" at first glance. However, much of the philosophy of Thai architecture is embedded in its form and function. Each house is of a different size and is composed of different materials, but all are interconnected by wooden walkways, much as the traditional Thai house on stilts was. They are all oriented towards the sea, and freely invite the natural setting into their interiors. The focal point is a long infinity-edge pool, with a large timber terrace that comes into its own as the sun sets gloriously over the horizon. It is here, as on the equivalent of the *chan-ban* verandah of old, that people congregate — the multi-functional space can be used to play, to eat, to chill, or to lounge.

Furthermore, in the same way that old Thai houses were at tune with nature, Villa Noi celebrates its natural setting at every turn. The owner, a Hong Kong businessman, wanted nature to take centre stage, so during the construction process great importance was placed on the preservation of the existing casuarina trees and the surrounding vegetation. Floor-to-ceiling glass doors and windows were designed to allow cool breezes to circulate around and through rooms. They also give views of the natural surrounds at every turn.

Bunnag is an architect who is often quoted elaborating upon the notion of Thai-ness or being Thai. He rightly points out that Thai culture has been informed and influenced by Indian, Chinese, Khmer and Burmese civilizations — and architecturally speaking a Thai pitched roof, or a Thai teak column could just as easily be identified as a Khmer one, for example. He therefore seeks to explain Thai-ness in his architecture in terms of experience — the way that spaces are integrated with nature to produce a relaxed experience; how interior and exterior areas merge into one for a carefree vibe. This concept of Thai *sabai sabai* (an expression that indicates wellbeing is paramount) is very evident at the relaxed and laid-back Villa Noi.

THIS PAGE AND PREVIOUS PAGE / Although modern in appearance, this contemporary home is traditional in attitude. This is because life here is lived in the in-between spaces — the areas that hover in the sphere between indoors and outdoors. And, if you are actually inside, it feels like you are outside because floor-to-ceiling windows and doors invite the natural surroundings into the home. Similarly, the materials are local wherever possible: walls of exposed brick, granite, and sustainable wood; flooring from sustainable wood and ceramic tiles.

LEFT AND RIGHT / For the most part interiors are integrated with the surrounding nature, using earth and wood tones in most rooms. There are even trees growing through the rooms in some places! A notable exception is in the modern kitchen. Here bright blush cupboard faces provide a statement-making splash of contrast at the centre of the project.

A Calm Serenity

This three-storey private residence, designed by Duangrit Bunnag of DBALP, is perched on a steep slope on the eastern coast of Phuket and boasts magnificent panoramic views over the sea. Utilising a palette of coffee and cream, it exudes a calm serenity.

The house is entered through a massive pivoted timber door set in a long grey granite-clad façade. On the outside there is no indication of the layered mass hidden inside — or of the ocean views beyond. The door opens into a narrow corridor that leads to a walkway over a narrow inner court complete with fountain, waterfall and reflecting pool. After that, one enters the house proper — and the dramatic view of sea, offshore islands and horizon is revealed. From here, one begins to descend. Transitioning between open and closed spaces, each area flows into the next in an effortless manner. Ample textural contrast in the form of exposed concrete, different stone finishes, teakwood and stainless steel is combined with lush, yet minimalist, décor. With the distant sea acting as a backdrop, the open-plan living room, kitchen and dining space that expands out to a glittering azure infinity-edge pool at the upper level is the heart of the home.

The client required two things: a full panoramic view of the sea and an integration with nature. The first was easily achieved, and the second is interpreted through Bunnag's selection of materials: cool limestone, smooth sandstone, granite, polished concrete, water and teakwood are all natural elements — and local to Thailand. Similarly, the experiential progression through the house allows one to savour the relationship between the architecture and its picturesque rural setting.

During the design and planning process, Bunnag was challenged with local regulations regarding

PREVIOUS PAGE, LEFT AND RIGHT BOTTOM / A gigantic centrally hinged wooden door in an exterior wall with a facade of uniform grey purposely underplays the drama that unfolds upon entering the house.

PREVIOUS PAGE, RIGHT TOP / The dining room with its super-sleek long table can be opened up to the pool deck, or enclosed in inclement weather.

OPPOSITE TOP / The multi-media room in shades of pale wood and cream overlooks a study room below.

OPPOSITE BELOW / Bedrooms and bathrooms espouse a cool tranquility; an adjacent pool and water feature, espansive views and luxe furnishings all contribute to the naturalistic ambiance.

RIGHT TOP / The narrow inner court separating the main mass of the house from its imposing exterior wall is cooled by a projectile fountain and pool.

RIGHT BELOW / Despite its size, the three-storey home almost seems to disappear into the surrounding landscape when viewed from afar.

height and perimeter restrictions. Instead of regarding these as obstacles, the architect found potential in the regulations which included a diagram of the hillside. He decided to transform the topology of the hill by turning it into a graphic form, a process he describes as "graphic topology". Nine graphic topological studies were produced before one was deemed suitable for the house design and the client's needs. To strengthen the hypothesis, a model of the building mass based on this final choice was created in order to get an overview of the form of the abstract spaces and their position on the various heights of the slope.

As such, the home has a singular geometry that is very appealing. It evokes a harmony between man and nature and a balance between the manmade and the natural environment — thereby fulfilling the client's desires and maintaining Thai ties with the land.

Urban Courtyard Home

Designed by one of Thailand's leading architects, Ajarn (Professor) Chulathat Kitibutr, this large courtyard house in prestigious Soi Thonglor off Sukhumvit Road in Bangkok is a marvel of form and function. Comprising two buildings — the foremost one containing three storeys and the one behind four — and an internal garden court, it utilizes many Thai forms realized in a thoroughly contemporary manner.

As in homes of old, both buildings have expansive balconies that run the length of the structures, and both are topped by roofs with large overhangs that help to protect from the tropical sun, wind and rain. As is sensible in the Thai climate, the floors of the balconies are covered in 30cm x 30cm slate tiles; cool underfoot, these reduce the temperature in hot, humid months. The balconies also provide pleasant outdoor spaces with casual tables and chairs to sit out on when the weather is pleasant.

Similarly, materials were chosen for both utilitarian and aesthetic purposes. The basic structure is made from concrete, a material that blocks noise and aids cooling, while the woodwork comes in a combination of two hardwoods — rosewood and teak. Both are highly durable, not to mention beautiful, with their shiny textures and evocative grains. The roof tiles are also made of concrete, but cast in a kite shape that both reflects Thai culture and is suitable for a property in a high-density area.

The layout of this elegant home is no less logical. The three-storey structure contains utilities at ground level, a relaxed living/dining room one floor up, and a large ceremonial Buddha hall and one bedroom on the top floor. The inner four-storey structure contains a kitchen at ground level, a formal living room on the first floor, a study and ensuite guest room above, and a huge master bedroom at the top. The owner, Khun Montri Virojnvechapant, an expert on authentic Thai cuisine and a columnist for some of Bangkok's leading lifestyle magazines, has designed all the interiors himself.

As befits his status and job, Khun Montri uses the home extensively for entertaining, so having both a formal and a more relaxed living/dining room comes in useful. While the former is all clean white and pristine, the latter sports a lively lime green, red and blue colour scheme. A combination of Italian furniture and Thai artefacts and artworks reflects a refined palate for the finer things in life. Naturally,

ABOVE / The internal courtyard that sits between the two-building home is leafy, cool and quiet. Here inbuilt seating in the form of benches, chairs and tables provides relaxed outdoor spaces for cool days; a similar principle was employed in homes of old.

OPPOSITE / One of the publications that Khun Montri contributes to is the Thai edition of Martha Stewart's home and lifestyle magazine — so it is only fitting that he has a discerning eye for interior *objets d'art*. From left to right: wooden puppet or *hun* of a Simian character from the *Ramakien*; a commemorative disc featuring the Thai king; beautifully carved betel set in coconut wood; detail of the Buddha Hall painting depicting mythological and real figures.

LEFT AND BELOW / The "relaxed" living room is a lively mix of colours and objects illuminated by some traditional gold-leaf, multi-tiered hanging lamps. Amongst the items on display are two puppets from the *Ramakien*, a number of family portraits and three traditional Thai pedestal fruit platters in foreground. The chairs set around the light-toned dining table are Philippe Starck Ghost chairs.

BELOW LEFT / A selection of items ranging from royal memorabilia to religious paraphernalia, as well as porcelains and ceramics are displayed in the shrine hall.

OPPOSITE / The more formal cream-toned living room features a mix of Italian and local furniture — Gervasoni sofas and De Padova dining chairs set around a locally made dining table. The two portraits are of HRH Princess Galyani Vadhana, while the Thai-style scrolls depict a reproduction of the biography of the Lord Buddha. The delicate porcelains on the coffee table in the foreground include some *bencharong* items and a couple of handmade ceramics from Japan.

the ceremonial hall dedicated to the Lord Buddha is one of the highlights of the home. In addition to an ornate altar, it features some intricate and finely detailed wall murals realized in traditional Sukhothai style by an award-winning young artist by the name of Khun Chuchart. As is fitting, they depict stories from the *Jatakas*, or the Life of the Buddha.

Ajarn Chulathat Kitibutr was awarded Thai National Artist status some years back and is probably best known for his design of the graceful Four Seasons Resort outside Chiang Mai. There he melded many Lanna or northern Thai architectural features into the creation of what is also a thoroughly modern resort. Here, in the home of Khun Montri, he has brought to fruition a very special structure. In his own words, he sums it up: "My inspiration for the Montri House was to capture the essence of Thai culture and aesthetics and also create something compatible with the owner's contemporary lifestyle." It appears he has achieved just that.

ABOVE / With one full-wall mural and a frieze around the upper rim of the room, this ceremonial hall dedicated to the Lord Buddha is both religious repository and a place for quiet contemplation. The teakwood ceiling with multi-tiered chandelier is particularly fine.

THAI ESCAPES

Thailand has long been renowned for its hospitality industry. Home to some stunning hotels that combine gorgeous surrounds with sunny weather, they have been soothing tired souls and rejuvenating the world-weary for decades. Today, the bar has been raised even higher as standards of service, harnessing the innate grace of the Thais, attains new levels.

This comes at an opportune moment, as visitors are increasingly seeking an escape from their stressful urban lives. They want personalised service, bespoke tours, specially constructed experiences that take them as far away as possible from their lives back home. This notion of a haven or hideaway in an exotic locale totally different from their everyday environment is what tropical dream-seekers desire. Be it a louche metropolitan oasis, a villa on the beach or a hangout in the hills, Thailand delivers. This is all the more so today as such hostelries epitimise the new Thai Style.

ABOVE / Carved wooden mannequin doubling up as a TCM acupressure point guide at Bangkok's innovative Siam hotel.

OPPOSITE / Bucolic vistas of Khao Yai National Park from a relaxation point in the boutique lodging of sala khaoyai.

An Airy Eyrie

Uniquely situated atop an elevated promontory on the northeast coast of Phuket, Point Yamu by COMO is part hotel, part art installation, part air, part light. A study in contrasts, the exterior is almost intimidating, certainly Brutalist, grey and utilitarian. The interior, on the other hand, soars with creativity.

Then there are the views: one side overlooks the limestone escarpments of Phang Nga Bay (made famous by James Bond's *The Man with the Golden Gun*); the other takes in views of the still waters and yet more islands of the Andaman Sea. With shimmering blue sea, sky and horizon nearly all round, the hotel and its attendant villas seem to float above the aqua seascape as if in a bubble.

One of COMO's Island Getaways, Point Yamu is designed with serious chilling in mind. There is a 100-metre long pool, a sybaritic COMO Shambala spa, two restaurants, a bar, and facilities for both children and teenagers. Across the bay, a dedicated beach club and private beach are the sole domain of hotel guests and the hotel is able and keen to host private events, meetings and the like.

Nonetheless, it is the hotel's interiors that really excite. Conceptualised and overseen by Italian furniture and textile designer Paola Navone, they are accomplished, quirky, sometimes sublimely beautiful, always interesting. Taking Thai-ness as her inspiration, Navone interprets this chameleon-like concept with imagination and originality. It's hard to believe that this is her first hotel project.

After a two-month orientation visiting the old streets and shophouses in Phuket Town, various temples and markets and other cultural sites, Navone consciously utilises Thai and Sino-Thai motifs and artefacts as a starting point for her design. Take the entrance lobby, for example. A gigantic space open on two sides, it is flanked by pillars clad in cracked tiles (a modernized version of the traditional cut-and-paste *chien-nien* frieze) and two floor-to-ceiling walls intricately decorated with boxy teakwood squares. Swaying lobster-trap lampshades cast light on an "altar" installation of stacked traditional *tang* tables decorated with Thai collectibles, while seating is loungy and slightly messy with artfully mussed-up Thai triangular cushions or *maun kwan*.

Other public spaces continue the theme: the Thai restaurant, accessed through a massive door with a Buddha hand handle, is decked out in the saffron tones of monks' robes and accented with a mosaic of golden fish. Outside a line of teak tree posts echoes the orange palette. The pool is lined with loungers

PREVIOUS PAGE, LEFT / Grey concrete corridors are enlivened with patterns of monks' alms bowls.

PREVIOUS PAGE, RIGHT / Trad Thai details are reinterpreted throughout the hotel, such as in the white linen triangular cushions (above) and the umbrella stands in the form of stone elephants, the informal symbol of the country (below).

ABOVE / Informal seating nook on a deck overlooking Phang Nga Bay.

LEFT / Turquoise and white are the predominant interior colours, a smart choice for a seaside hotel. Ceramic tiles are all individually hand fired to Navone's specifications and have an iridescent sparkle in the glaze. Lighting is similarly individualistic — many lights double as artworks in themselves.

TOP / Paying homage to her roots, Navone has styled La Sirena, the international restaurant, with an Italian pizzazz. Behind the pizza oven on the left is a long bar that features a back wall hung with white crockery. Rattan hanging lightshades add a local twist.

ABOVE / Detail from a cracked tile column covering; texture is as important as colour and fit here.

separated by umbrellas, the stands of which are fashioned from stone elephants — Thailand's *de facto* symbol. Elsewhere, in corridors and corners, one finds a variety of Thai-style installations: a wall of hanging garlands or *malai*; a feature made from Lanna tribal pom-poms; graphic depictions of offering bowls; and a ceiling covered with an abstracted Buddhist *yantra* pattern. These serve to illuminate slightly dark and mysterious corridors, acting as focal points in what would otherwise be somewhat sombre walkways.

And, of course, after dark comes illumination. Stepping from one of these murky corridors into a room or suite, one literally finds the light at the end of the tunnel. Offering a full spectrum of turquoise, teal and white, all 79 suites and rooms are gossamer-light in character and tone. Ceramic wall dividers and floor tiles are a twist on those found in Sino-Chinese shophouses, while the aqua palette is refreshing and lively. Many have private plunge pools with sparkling cobalt tiles, while bathrooms are sleek and contemporary. As is to be expected, the one-, two- and three-bedroom villas are equally tasteful. Less colourful than the rooms and sporting an ice-cool, white-on-white scheme, they nonetheless entice with fresh, clean interiors.

In fact, the calculated contrast between grey concrete exteriors and exuberant, airy interiors is sexy and successful throughout. Architecture by Jean-Michel Gathy with its mix of twisted metal and resolutely grey concrete is deliberately imposing, intimidating even. Its consciously masculine aesthetic is sensitively softened inside by the feminine, Italian-chic touch of Paola Navone.

ABOVE / The welcoming, yet slightly unorthodox, lobby features a central "altar" of stacked Thai *tang* laden with everyday items found in Thailand. It acts as a good talking point for a journey round the hotel.

OPPOSITE TOP / Examples of some of the installation-type decorations found in the hotel: a hanging artwork with woollen pom-poms as made by the Hmong tribe in northern Thailand; cute carp, fish revered for their supposed ability to confer longevity and luck, "swimming" on a wall; a Buddha's hand in the *vitarka mudra* doubles up as a door handle.

OPPOSITE BELOW / Two giant frescoes of gold-and-red swimming fish with pendant transparent bubble lights and a gold-leaf wall make a striking statement in Nahmyaa, the resort's Thai restaurant.

LEFT / As Mies van der Rohe once remarked "God is in the details", an apt phrase when considering Navone's attention to detail throughout the resort. Clockwise from top left: close-up of one of the lobby's wood walls shows the intricacy of the workmanship; a giant piece of wood is sliced to form a table cum sculpture with ceramic decoration; Tracey Emin-esque signage on a corridor wall; a piece of salvaged wood is an item of beauty in its own right; a wall covering resembling both the tiles of a traditional Thai roof and the gills of a fish; whimsical hanging wood artwork.

OPPOSITE / Custom-crafted tiles in sparkling shades characterise the sybaritic bathrooms in the spa, rooms and villas. Glass lights and mirrors are decorative as well as utilitarian.

A Taste of Old Siam

Owned by the Sukosol family, well-known both in Thailand and abroad as art collectors, philanthropists and hoteliers, the Siam Hotel is the product of a creative collaboration between Bangkok-based designer Bill Bensley and director Krissada Sukosol Clapp. Set on close to three acres of family land in the Dusit area with prime Chao Phraya river frontage, the hotel is a tasteful mix of sybaritic Old Siam and Art Deco glamour. For a relaxing retreat from hectic Bangkok, there is no place else like it.

History seeps through all aspects of the hotel. A Thai-style vibe mixes and mingles with colonial, Chinese and hothouse-chic accents for an Oriental

ABOVE / An ancient Chinese statue marking acupressure points for a Traditional Chinese Medicine doctor is part of the owner's collection.

RIGHT / Drawing inspiration from the Musée d'Orsay, the Main Residence is in effect a huge glasshouse. Suites, lining both sides of the reflecting pool, are airy and light.

ABOVE / An airy court in the main building has a Spanish Revival or Moorish feel, with soothing central water feature and fresh plantings.

OPPOSITE / Inspired by the Art Deco style that was popular during the reign of King Rama V, interiors were designed by Bill Bensley. Dark woods, leather and metallic accents are well matched with the owner's extensive collection that includes vintage maps, Ming and Tang ceramics, an old bicycle, and more.

opulent feel. On entering, the Main Residence, a seamless combination of indoor and outdoor courts and galleries, sets the scene. Built to reflect the grand style of the King Rama V period (r 1868–1910), there are Classical proportions in the architecture and Art Deco accents in the interiors. A muted monochrome scheme with texture in the form of wood, weave, leather and stone is the perfect backdrop for Sukosol Clapp's extensive art collection. Eastern antiques in the form of oversized teak apothecary cabinets and opium beds sit on cool stone floors, while display cases house priceless *objets d'art* such as 18th-century Chinese ceramics salvaged from old galleon shipwrecks.

Elsewhere, there are numerous vitrines holding multiple curios and wares, original Pan-Am posters of Thailand, dark pools and lush landscaping, as well as life-sized antique statues and turn-of-the-century artworks. This is truly a museum-worthy collection, more like an art installation than a hotel lobby. As

LEFT / The Chao Praya is visible from this elevated walkway that connects the Thai houses that comprise restaurant and bar. The walkway mimics the *chan-ban* platform of the traditional Thai house.

OPPOSITE TOP / Decked out with old folding wood-and-velvet cinema seats, the private screening room plays host to movie nights, guest lectures and clips on Thailand's history.

OPPOSITE BELOW / The blissful Opium Spa is a restorative space with not a chemical product in sight.

well as multiple lounges and relaxation nooks, there is an authentic *muay* Thai boxing gym, a sybaritic subterranean spa, and a decent sized screening room with vintage cinema chairs. Facilities are as inspired — and inspiring — as the collections all around.

This main building also houses 28 suites, each with a colonial-style internal verandah, while ten further pool villas located closer to the river are an amalgam of Thai, Chinese and colonial influences. Think heavy woods, Ming-style consoles, scholar's chairs, archival artworks and boxy leather trunks, all reflecting Thailand's multi-cultural history, as well as salvaged teak doors and wrought-iron spiral staircases. The latter lead up to private rooftop terraces, perfect for pre-dinner cocktails or secluded sunbathing. The final suite is housed in a century-old teakwood house sourced from Ayutthaya by Jim Thompson for Connie Mangskau, a Thai-American socialite whose exotic parties were the toast of the town in Bangkok's post-War years.

Whether you're imbibing sunset drinks on the hotel pier, learning the intricacies of Thai pomelo and glass noodle salad in a cooking class, stretching sinews in the lap pool, or partaking of a post-prandial cigar in the teak house dining room, you'll be experiencing present-day Thai culture — albeit it with a nostalgic feel — at first hand. And the historic sites and culture of Old Siam, the museums, palaces and riverfront mansions, are a boat ride away. Take a tour with your own private guide.

ABOVE / Whichever accommodation option you choose, you'll be pampered by a private butler in luxurious surrounds. This suite features an Art Deco bedhead and old Chinese scrolls on the walls.

LEFT / Chinese elements, such as this antique pair of heavy doors and expansive day bed, welcome guests in the anteroom of a pool villa.

RIGHT / All palatial rooms and suites are impossibly romantic, while bathrooms sport black-and-white colonial-style tiling and Art Deco lights.

Contemporary meets Colonial

Formerly the Chedi, this stylish resort — now under management of Anantara — boasts an enviable position right on the serene Ping River but just steps away from Chiang Mai's famed night market and Sunday Walking Street. Designed by Kerry Hill, one of Singapore's foremost architects, it comprises a reception pavilion and accommodation blocks constructed around what was once the British Consulate. This handsome colonial-style building

dating from the 1920s houses the hotel's restaurant and is given pride of place within the compound.

In many ways the Anantara Chiang Mai epitomizes the character of the town where it is located. This venerable walled city was once the capital of the ancient Lanna kingdom and is filled with ancient *wats*, splendid stupas and saffron-robed monks. But it's also a thriving tourist hub with a sometimes frenetic pace — there's a plethora of cosmopolitan restaurants, hotels, galleries, shops and markets all vying for business. The hotel mimics this old/new contradiction: the design of the accommodations is sleek and contemporary, yet the restaurant building harks back to an earlier era.

Hill purposefully turned his back on the cityscape and oriented the hotel towards the river. On entering the main entrance lobby, there are framed views of the Consulate building, while the accommodations

ABOVE LEFT / The 1920s Consulate building is typical of its era: expansive wrap-around verandahs and deep eaves invite in air and protect from sun and rain. The building has been sensitively renovated and furnished with heavy wooden tables and chairs.

ABOVE RIGHT / A large reflecting pool and lawn (partially seen on the left) separates one of the new four-storey accommodation blocks from the old building housing the restaurant.

wrap around the exterior fringes of the site. The spa building and swimming pool are placed within the interior courtyard and lie adjacent and parallel to the river. This ensures that the experience bestowed by the architecture and layout within the compound is quiet and contemplative.

Detached timber-clad screens and corridors shield the 85 guestrooms from the urban chaos on the perimeter, and each room is accessed through a light-filled private court. Even though the timber screens are resolutely modern and deliberately unornamented, they do reference those found in traditional Thai houses. They also encourage cross-ventilation of cooling air and act as noise buffers.

Each of the luxe guestrooms boasts a balcony with a double day-bed that overlooks the gardens, thereby enlarging already decent-sized rooms. Similarly, floor-to-ceiling windows invite in both light and views. Furniture and fittings are all crafted from local materials — hardwood floors, hand-made red glazed wall tiles, terrazzo plinths and teak and rattan furniture. While the style may be contemporary, the materials are rooted in the immediate Chiang Mai locality.

LEFT / Beautiful river views are to be had at the 34-metre-long, streamlined swimming pool, a few metres from the water's edge. Chargoal-grey loungers, white umbrellas, lily ponds and stands of manicured reeds complete the scene.

RIGHT / An upper-floor balcony with rattan seating has delightful river views.

BELOW / A River View Suite combines wood with a grey and pink palette. The bed runner and cushions feature a hill tribe weave, while paper and metal lights are designed to reflect the traditional paper umbrellas and lanterns found in the north of Thailand around Chiang Mai.

On the Veranda

Set within an ancient teak forest and overlooking an agricultural landscape of tea plantation, ricefield and longan orchard with magnificent views of the Sameung Mountains, the Veranda Chiang Mai is an exquisite rural retreat. With sister properties in Hua Hin and Pattaya, Veranda is a name to watch out for.

Designed by Smith Obayawat of the Bangkok Architect Co Ltd, with landscaping by Belt Collins International and interiors by August Design Consultant, the primary focus of the hotel is its setting. Verawat Ongvasith, President of Veranda Resort and Spa, explains that he was inspired by a trip to Bali where he saw a great many quality resorts in mountainous areas. When he found the hotel's rural site some half hour's drive from Chiang Mai, he knew it was the place for his next hotel. "Some of Bali's magnificent resorts are not close to the beach at all .... (they are) designed to fit with the atmosphere of the mountains. Even when raining they look spectacular." This was what he had in mind for the Veranda Chiang Mai.

The overall design concept sees the rooms, villas, pool and stand-alone restaurant almost as a "town" surrounded by forest and fields. To that end, it is

encircled by a brick wall which mimics the ancient walled city of Chiang Mai. On arrival, a corridor of polished concrete cooled by falling water greets the visitor and opens into an inner court containing grey-tiled pools, an open-air restaurant and three low-rise buildings housing 69 guest rooms, all with balconies or patios and several with plunge pools. These various structures are separated by a series of courtyards, terraces and reflective pools all over-looking stepped rice and tea plantations with framed views out to the mountains beyond. A range of local materials — locally quarried stone, pebbles, wooden tree trunks — mixes with concrete and brick to produce a serene ambience.

Khun Somwang Leevanijkul of Belt Collins explains the ethos behind the landscaping: "Historically the Thai garden is more in tune with agriculture, as opposed to the man-made Japanese or Chinese garden. We used the simplicity of Thailand's rural landscape as a distinction because our project is rooted locally." To that end he retained all the existing trees and shrubs, trained plants, creepers and climbers to clamber over roofs, and carved undulating furrows in the rice fields. The result is a carefully interwoven merging of landscape, cultural artifacts and architecture.

Water, too, is an important element, with various streams, plunge pools, waterways and channels running throughout the resort. Fittingly, the infinity-edge swimming pool, elevated to gain prominence, seems to float above the existing topography. It is clearly the resort's centrepiece — and offers enticing views of the surrounding panorama.

PREVIOUS PAGE / The elevated pool lined with turquoise-grey tiles features a central grassy deck. It is perfectly positioned at the centre of the resort with vistas of the surrounding hills.

OPPOSITE / Plunge pool pavilions include a living area at the foot of the bed that is tastefully furnished in a combo of cream, rust and taupe with scatter cushions in hill tribe fabrics.

ABOVE / The roof of the attractive timber-and-concrete accommodation blocks is slightly upturned, so as to allow rainwater to flow back.

ABOVE AND OPPOSITE / Concrete, wood and brick were the main materials used in construction. Interspersed with generous water bodies, the idea is for guests to experience an aspect of Lanna culture. The history of Chiang Mai is also deemed an important part of the overall guest experience.

A Haven of Calm

The Rachamankha, an atmospheric hotel within the ancient walls of Chiang Mai, is calm, collected and serene, a veritable retreat from the city's sometimes frenetic pace. Combining stand-alone buildings and pavilions with garden spaces, it is airy, quiet and uncluttered. In many ways, its hallowed halls, cool courts and stone-paved cloisters mimic those found in ancient monasteries and religious sanctuaries of the past.

This is somewhat apt, as one of the rooms with its multi-tiered roofs in the main quadrangle is influenced by the highly individualistic *viharn* (preaching hall) of Wat Phra That Lampang Luang in Lampang Province; but there are also ancient vernacular Chinese influences in the layout and interiors elsewhere. Comprising three earthen brick-laid courtyards, low-rise, colonnaded buildings and a central pavilion-style lounge, the hotel also adheres to Chinese *feng shui* principles. The basic construction is of earthen bricks covered with white limestone plaster, while walls thrust out in the ancient manner. Set in a walled compound, the Rachamankha's architecture enables guests to really experience — feel and touch — genuine Lanna culture. It appears that this was the owner's primary aim.

The architect, Ong-ard Satrabhandhu, is a Thai whose designs often include the use of classical and traditional vocabulary. He believes that buildings should be appropriate for their history, climate and setting — and one of his overriding concerns is architectural preservation. In particular he is working with officials and like-minded professionals in the cultural conservation of Lanna religious architecture. Heavily influenced by the Mon and Khmer peoples, but with an absorption of styles from China, Burma and Laos from the 13th century onwards, Lanna *wats* and associated buildings can be stark and simple, yet overwhelmingly beautiful. Many of Satrabhandhu's designs have a similar aesthetic.

Because of its construction methods, the hotel complex is almost monastic in ambience. Where it isn't austere, however, is in the service and amenities:

OPPOSITE / One of a pair of Ming dynasty lion statues that guard an interior courtyard.

RIGHT / A pair of massive doors leads to an internal courtyard lined with hand-made earthen bricks. The hanging lantern has influences from both Art Deco and Lanna temple design, while the tassel is typically Chinese.

there's a gorgeous 20-metre swimming pool; a lofty restaurant with paintings depicting the Lord Buddha's life, sober Ming-style chairs and large Lanna lanterns serving extremely tasty Lanna, Burmese and Shan cuisine; an adjacent bar; massage on demand; and very attentive staff. And even though rooms are simple, these are no monks' cells. With 18 superior and four deluxe rooms as well as one two-bedroom suite, each is different. Furnished with one-off antiques scoured from the region, bamboo blinds, Burmese art and Chinese porcelain lamps, latticed windows and vintage furniture, they are accessed via an antique door with ornate handle and wooden bolts.

Other notable features are a library with over 2,000 books, a gallery showcasing some of the Lanna Kingdom's finest art and antiquities, a red-pillared pavilion lounge and peaceful gardens. Even though you are within the old walled city a stone's throw from Wat Phra Singh and a 15-minute walk from the Night Bazaar, you'll feel far removed from Chiang Mai's hectic streets. As one guest put it: "As soon as you enter, you leave the city behind. You are in the city, but not of the city."

OPPOSITE TOP / The hotel is filled with antiques collected by owner Rooj Changtrakul over the years. Antique Chinese windows with lathed wooden bars allow air to circulate freely.

OPPOSITE BELOW / Multi-tiered roofs and colonnaded verandahs fronting the guest suites draw their inspiration from Lanna temple design. The spaces between the buildings are considered as important as the buildings themselves.

ABOVE / The Lanna-inspired exterior of the wing that houses the hotel's bar and restaurant is fronted by a low hedge and topiary bushes. Red lithographs by Robert Motherwell hanging behind the bar can be seen through the door.

ABOVE / Most Thai compounds include a spirit house in the form of a miniature traditional Thai house with a small porch on which offerings are placed to appease the spirits of the land where the dwelling is built.

RIGHT TOP / The internal courtyard of the restaurant, with blue-and-white ceramics both in display cases and on the walls, is a tranquil and atmospheric place to dine al fresco.

RIGHT BELOW / Titles in the convivial, yet contemplative, library range from novels to works on Thai history, art, architecture, design and culture, while the spa, overlooking the teal-tiled pool, features outdoor massage beds.

LEFT / A guest suite features a Chinese scroll painting above the bed, heavy antique furniture in dark wood and cool terracotta tiles underfoot.

OPPOSITE / Massive lacquered solid teak columns stretch up to the double- or triple-height ceiling in the lobby. Here, the roof structure is inspired by Chiang Mai temple architecture. Beneath the lofty roof, a contemporary Thai table holds a vast vat of white orchids.

A Treasury for Book-Lovers

When you pull up at The Library in Koh Samui, you'd be well advised to ponder on the old adage "don't judge a book by its cover". For the hotel's small reception building and unassuming forecourt belie the jewel that lies behind.

It's only when you start to walk into the compound that you realize what lies before you: a series of white-on-white cubic buildings set within a quiet garden shaded by trees starts the processional route. As one progresses, the eye alights on a deep crimson swimming pool at the shore end with pristine blue sea behind. It is more than eye-catching; no artist could conjure such a painterly scene.

But it's not just the pool, extraordinary as it is, that attracts repeat visitors. A sophisticated breed of sybarites has consistently returned to this hotel for its aesthetic, its guest experience and its relative quiet at the southern end of Chaweng Beach.

Part of the Design Hotels group and open since 2007, The Library sits in relative isolation on this busy beach. The brainchild of Samui native Kasemtham Sornsong who created the hotel with designer Tirawan Songsawat, the basic concept centres round books: The lobby is the Contents, rooms are Pages, the suite is called Bookmark and the restaurant is aptly named The Page. The hotel's library, with a collection of over 1,300 books provides the "glue" that binds the whole together. Sornsong, an avid reader, explains: "We invite our guests to become the writers of their own personal stories while staying with us. The Library can thus be likened to a book of clean white pages, waiting to be filled with colourful characters and fantastic adventures."

Even though the overall design is conceptually contemporary and Western, a number of small yet significant details reveal distinct Thai sensibilities. Sornsong explains: "Our minimal architectural style, for example, stems from the belief that simplicity is tantamount to true sophistication and that achieving

ABOVE / Two views of the library at The Library. "I believe that the book, being a repository of stories and experiences, is immortal," says the owner. "Personally, I'm a fan of paper books. A section of our library (which we call The Lib) is from my personal collection — mostly art and design books." Guests are welcome to borrow or purchase books at any time.

ABOVE AND OPPOSITE TOP / The Library's owner, Kasemtham Sornsong, answers a question about the pool with another question: "When asked 'Why Red?', I often joke with a counter-question, 'Why not?'." Fair enough, you may say, but when pressed further, he elaborates: "It only takes a simple idea and a slight variation from the ordinary to transform the mundane into something truly spectacular." And, no doubt, spectacular, the pool certainly is.

LEFT / Early-morning breakfast served to couples on mattresses on the sand is a tranquil affair. Even though the beach has expanded steadily over the years, this southern section is more sedate than other areas, and much of the charm of old Samui still remains.

ABOVE / One of 10 impressions of The Reader relaxing by the sea (with a book of course!). Designed and made by the artist Tirawan Songsawat, who is also the hotel's designer, the sculptures are composed from fibreglass resin. Manufactured in Bangkok, they were transported to the island and placed in different poses at various locations around the resort grounds.

happiness is not complicated at all. This philosophy harks back to the old carefree days of island life in Samui and is a concept shared by many locals. Another important aspect of the design is our culture's respect for the land. During the early phases of The Library's construction, the trees endemic to the property posed a bit of a challenge. I wanted to maintain the integrity of the existing nature, so bulldozers were out of the question. In the end, it was the trees that dictated the overall layout of the hotel. All structures were created to blend in with them."

Sornsong was also keen to use a lot of wood in the design, offsetting cool concrete with warm wood in shutters, furniture and floors. Oversized rooms are a hedonist's delight: with floor-to-ceiling glass inviting the outdoors in, each features an elevated platform resembling that of a traditional Thai house. This mixed-use area houses bed, seating and dining table, and affords views into the tranquil garden or over the sea.

But whichever way you look, your eye will always be drawn back to the stunning swimming pool, sparkling with its mosaic of small orange, yellow and red tiles made in Italy. The hue changes as the sun moves. "I find it the perfect centrepiece between the stark white structures of our accommodation units and the pastel blue of the sea," says Sornsong. "The boldness of its colour speaks of passion and energy. It also portrays our enthusiasm to captivate and think outside the box."

ABOVE / The Library offers a choice from 26 studio cabins and suites, meaning the hotel never gets over-crowded. Interiors are tranquil with clean lines and cool black, white and red interiors inviting guests to curl up with a favourite book. Texture and touch are crucial too with the warmth of wood contrasting with the cooler concrete and steel found elsewhere in the rooms.

OPPOSITE / The resort features two chic restaurants, one fronting the beach called The Page and this one next to the entrance called Drink Gallery. As it faces Chaweng Beach Road, it takes on a bit of the character of the street in its design. There's a medley of seating, while a central high table at the centre seats up to 14 people. Overall the feeling is playful, yet still arty.

A Hillside Hideaway

A member of SALA Hospitality Group, a boutique hotel company in Thailand, the focus at sala khaoyai is on the surrounding countryside. Perched dramatically on a scenic hilltop over-looking Khao Yai National Park, there are two options: do nothing at all except pamper yourself or go pell-mell for outdoor activities such as hiking, mountain biking, bird-watching and the like.

Offering only seven rooms and suites, living isolated with nature is the over-riding theme at sala khaoyai. All bedrooms are partially carved into the hillside, thereby offering a slightly "underground" atmosphere, while panoramic views are to be had from the main building and infinity-edge swimming pool above. In fact, when you arrive at sala khaoyai, you are confronted by 138 steps — there's no way round them, you have to climb up to the resort. You're rewarded on arrival though: the views over the surrounding parkland are breathtaking.

The owner of sala khaoyai has given over less than one tenth of his land to the hotel, reserving the rest for cultivation of five different species of tree — mahogany, teak, rubber, hardwood *makha*, prized for its beautiful patina, and *takhian (Hopea odorata)*. Thais believe that the latter tree is inhabited by a sylvan tree spirit, so the tree cannot be felled. Be that as it may, there is no doubt that the tree-planting endeavour is contributing to Khao Yai's ozone quality — currently, it is ranked seventh in the world.

Other sustainable features at the resort include the use of sea-salt instead of chlorine to maintain cleanliness in the swimming pool and delicious food grown in the hotel's own organic gardens. Sitting in the open-air hilltop restaurant, with an outdoor wood-burning fireplace on the deck and 360-degree views over the surrounding rolling hills and valleys, is deeply satisfying. Solitude and stillness, broken only by the sounds of breeze and birdsong, are a wonderful panacea for stressed urbanites.

PREVIOUS PAGE / In keeping with the Nature theme, wood and water are key in the resort. Out of the seven accommodations, there are two sala pool villas and two one-bedroom pool villa suites. Each has its own private swimming pool and fireplace for cooler, winter evenings. In addition, the resort's main swimming pool affords spectacular sunset views.

ABOVE LEFT AND RIGHT / A décor palette of coffee-and-cream with hints of mint and taupe in the accommodations is entirely in keeping with the fresh feeling in the resort. Natural wood, local stone, leather and pristine linens all contribute to the open, yet intimate, rooms. Bathrooms are particularly impressive with sinks carved from a single block of heavy golden stone.

A Real Treasure

As Koh Samui and Koh Phangan become ever more built up, some of the surrounding islands are beginning to be "discovered" by enterprising individuals, perhaps seeking to reconstruct the idyllic days when the islands in the Gulf of Thailand were largely undeveloped. In the old days, a hut with no electricity and limited running water in a relatively secluded environment was within the reach of every enterprising traveller. Today, it appears that people want more: they want an "escape", but they still require some creature comforts.

Preferably these should include decent plumbing, air-conditioning, tasty food and other amenities, but should be presented in a pristine environment where the downsides of civilization haven't arrived. Ergo, the surrounds need to be wild, untamed and "untouched", even as the immediate environment is bug-free, clean and sanitized. And if all this can be realized with a light environmental footprint, so much the better.

PREVIOUS PAGE AND OPPOSITE / At the centre of the resort is a black limestone swimming pool surrounded by eight tented villas, the interiors of which contain a beautiful, black limestone tub set on a bed of pebbles.

LEFT / Other accommodations are an attractive combination of wood and white. Keeping things simple is key at The Treasure.

BELOW / Beachside villas with small plunge pools afford many venues from which to enjoy the numerous views from either side of the island. One side opens onto a white sand beach, the other an untouched coral reef, perfect for snorkeling and diving.

If this sounds like a tall order, one need look no further than a ten-minute boat ride from Koh Samui's southern tip to a resort called The Treasure on the neighbouring island of Koh Mudsum. Opened in mid 2013, the resort spans from one side of the island to the other, and is the only place to stay — thus far.

With 37 villas and rooms, the design incorporates local materials such as teak and bamboo, but there are also some limestone, marble and modern fixtures and fittings. During construction, utmost importance was placed on preserving the existing environment with no trees being felled. Forward-looking technology in the form of a water treatment system that allows for water to be reused for multiple purposes means that no waste water is discharged into the sea. Also, water heaters use heat expelled from the air-conditioners instead of electricity to produce hot water. Such sensitivity to the impact of running the resort is a hallmark of The Treasure's approach.

A desire for privacy while reconnecting with nature seems to be a global phenomenon — especially among people who live in cities and have busy work lives. However, such guests are also well informed about "bad tourist practice" and do not want to kill the golden goose that they are experiencing, as it were. Thailand is well placed to provide relaxation and recreation in pristine surrounds — and The Treasure is a prime example of how this may be provided and packaged in a sustainable and responsible manner.

LIVING WITH NATURE

Traditional Thai dwellings were always intimately connected to the environment. Constructed entirely of wood and raised high on stilts, they varied between a few and many buildings linked by open terraces. Often surrounded by trees with water in the form of a river or *klong* close by, they invited the outdoors in. In the 20th century, the advent of air-conditioning and the growth of urban conurbations resulted in many Thais abandoning such forms for condominiums, apartment blocks and self-contained units.

Fortuitously, recent times have seen architects and landscape designers keen to reconnect with the natural environment, and an increasing number of homes once again display key aspects of the archetypal Thai house. Whether this comes in the form of indoor/outdoor living, use of materials, certain design elements, or the integration of pool, river or sea into the home is irrelevant. What is encouraging is that such structures are more often than not geared towards a sustainable model of development and maintenance — and the beauty of Thailand's stunning scenery is invited to take centre stage again.

ABOVE / A cool pool reflects the sunset on a Bangkok penthouse deck.

OPPOSITE / A relaxing day bed at the Sedhapura resort in Thailand's north east overlooks the Mekong river to Laos.

Among the Rocks of Santikhiri

Santikhiri is an emerging estate of homes and villas on the island of Koh Samui that sets great store by its natural environment. Situated on more than 25 acres of coconut plantation and granite escarpments overlooking the ocean, there are currently 19 houses already built, with ten plots awaiting ownership. Caves, ancient ficus trees, palms and magnificent boulders, not to mention gorgeous sea and forest views, characterize the pristine surrounds.

Because of its eco philosophy, the estate has attracted a number of like-minded people, all of whom have built unusual homes. Originally, some ten years ago, because there was a more or less common approach espoused towards building only very basic design guidelines were imposed, such as a footprint limit of 16 percent and a height limit of 12 metres. However, as houses started to come up, a great diversity of styles and attitudes became apparent. The footprint limit was increased to 20 percent to be in line with neighbouring developments, and there has been a general move towards bigger and more elaborate structures. The community is now developing more detailed design and construction guidelines in order to maintain the natural environment that makes this housing estate so special.

The house we feature here is completely inspired by the extraordinary character of the site that entranced the owners, Godelieva Aerts and Robert Powell, at first sight. "We saw that one

needed to build something that was also way out of the ordinary," explains Powell, an architect, "Something that could, if possible, emphasise the unique sense of place and the extreme nature of the setting — the rocks, the trees, and so on."

As such, the aim was to incorporate the site's boulders and trees in such a way that they would become fundamental elements of the house, even though at the outset there was no solid plan as to how this might be achieved. However, as design and construction began, the structure fell into place: three "rooms" following the natural contours of the land formed three separate pavilions — a main living/dining room, a studio/guest room and a master bedroom. Entrance to the main living room is through a steep and narrow gap in the rocks, and a series of terrazzo and pebblewash steps and pathways connect the various spaces. The built floor area is about 200 square metres in total.

Powell explains their home as built metaphors for the basic forms of shelter in the tropics: spreading branches that shade, cool recesses of caves that protect. As such, the division between interior and exterior spaces is blurred, to an extent where the home becomes part of the living, breathing landscape in which it is embedded. The resultant lifestyle is consequently "truly living as one with Nature".

PREVIOUS PAGE LEFT / Acrylic on linen paintings in niches in the rocks are of *dakinis* or Tibetan "sky walkers" and are copies of images in a 15th-century temple in Mustang, Nepal.

PREVIOUS PAGE RIGHT / A massive boulder becomes a backrest for this lounging area decorated in the ochre and rust tones of monks' robes. The Buddha image is a reproduction in bronze from a Thai company.

ABOVE / Terrazzo surfaces and copper sinks feature in the bathrooms where an open-to-the-elements ethos is paramount. The bathroom adjacent the kitchen has a huge ficus tree growing in it.

PREVIOUS PAGE LEFT / A set of steps between two large boulders leads into the main living/dining room with kitchen incorporated. The roof structure is made of small section elements, 10cm diameter steel columns and 5cm x 10cm timber trusses, so the surface has a detailed fineness of textures, like the underfoliage of a large tree. Once inside, cozy shelter provided by trees is the inspiration. Smooth terrazzo floors are cool underfoot and through flow of air is plentiful. The living/lounging area is centre and right on an elevated platform, while a dining table and kitchen counter are at left. The kitchen worktop, made from a large slab of old hardwood sourced from a boat-building yard in the south of Thailand, is supported on blocks of laterite stone. The same stone is used for the wall behind the kitchen. The dining table is a piece of woodchip board impregnated with cement. The surface was painted and ragged with oil paint many times, to give a rich, deep colour and texture.

OPPOSITE / The master bedroom gives a whole new interpretation to sleeping with nature in the tropics. The four-metre-high ceiling doubles up as a viewing platform and nine glass blocks embedded in the heavily insulated roof slab allow sunlight to filter through. A huge granite boulder forms the back wall and water is allowed to trickle down its surface via a copper pipe giving sustenance to lichen growing here. When the fans are switched on, the wet rock face becomes a natural air cooler.

ABOVE / All copper doors, light shades and sinks were made on site by local carpenters and guttering fabricators, using full size cardboard models provided by the owners. The beautiful patina comes from many experiments. This particular bathroom door was made in the cross section shape of an aerofoil or a flattened oval to fit the space.

RIGHT / A small garden terrace overlooking the beach and islands below is sheltered and shaded by friendly massive rocks and native trees. It is the perfect spot for a morning coffee.

ABOVE / The massive viewing platform above the master bedroom is breezy and cool and affords outstanding views. As is to be expected, the boulders and trees are integral to the overall design.

Spa in the Forest

Even though the inception of this ground-breaking spa facility dates back to the 1980s, in many ways its philosophy encapsulates a new approach to development in Thailand. Gone are the days when the environment played second fiddle to rampant growth, when bricks and mortar rampaged roughshod over the natural environment. For the owners of Tamarind Springs Forest Spa believed (and still do believe) that a gentle, low-impact approach is the only way to both meet the needs of their customers and to maintain their site's intrinsic natural beauty.

At a time when Koh Samui's tourist industry was experiencing a period of rapid, unplanned expansion, the partners at Tamarind Springs were extolling the virtues of slow growth. It's a credit to them that they built carefully and organically, all the while protecting their one hugely powerful asset — the unique natural environment in which their spa is set.

Located in the island's hinterland on the site of an old coconut plantation "peopled" with huge granite boulders thrown up by past tectonic shifts, the spa utilizes the area's natural spring-fed pools, rocks and trees in its offering. Large steam rooms, housing Thai herbal saunas with lemongrass, lime and other exotic ingredients, are found where two mighty boulders meet. Spring-fed dipping pools with icy, invigorating water are open to the elements, while airy massage pavilions on stilts are dotted around the secluded hillside setting.

The project started in the late 1980s with the construction of some simple villas with open-air bathrooms and decks. Detlef Dirksen, one of the

PREVIOUS PAGE AND ABOVE / When formulating the various pools, walkways and buildings, the existing contours of the site were always respected — and retained. This singular approach resulted in the Green Leaf Foundation awarding Tamarind Springs Forest Spa a 5 Leaf certificate, the highest of its rankings, in January 2012. The foundation, a joint initiative by Thailand's Tourism Authority, the United Nations Environment Program and others, promotes standards for the tourism industry through environmental assessment and audit programmes. As such, it is often seen as a benchmark for sustainable planning and development.

founding partners, explains: "My philosophy is that, in a unique and stunningly beautiful hillside setting like the one which is home to Tamarind Springs, spaces for human habitation should as much as possible be made integrated parts of the existing surrounding environment." As a result, the villas appear to have grown naturally as an integral part of the ecology of the site. Individually designed and appointed, each is different. In one, the bedroom may be built up against the side of a rockface, in another a giant ficus tree may sprout up through the outside bathroom.

As the owners note: "The awareness, behaviours and processes that drive our eco-vision have always been in place: they cover the whole spectrum of operations, from the use of building materials, water, electricity, and locally sourced food ingredients, to the unobtrusive and gentle way we have developed the lush property." The result is a peaceful, tropical retreat that respects and protects its environment, thereby allowing visitors to truly reconnect with the slow measured beat of the natural world. As a result such customers often return to their lives nurtured, refreshed and revitalized.

LEFT / For the villas, the ethos is all about openness and merging the outdoors with the indoors. There are large open deck areas, glass panelled sliding doors opening up entire walls, open-to-the-sky bathrooms, and even semi-open kitchens. "In order not to support the ongoing destruction of tropical rain forests, at Tamarind Springs we decided many years ago to only use recycled timber from old houses and/or aged coconut wood," explains Dirksen. As such, the accommodations were built with such wood and plastered brick, and used thatch or tile for roofing materials.

ABOVE / Exterior floors exposed to sun and rain, for example in bathrooms and public areas, are composed of mostly natural stones and tiles.

A Penthouse in Bangkok

Situated on a bend in the Chao Phraya river on the Thonburi side, this duplex penthouse apartment affords almost 360 degree views of the surrounding attractions on both sides of the river. The Grand Palace and the Temple of the Dawn are clearly visible in the distance, while closer to home is a bird's eye view of the roofs of Wat Thon Noppakhun, an old monastery and temple, almost directly below.

Consisting of five bedrooms, four bathrooms and a guest powder room, magnificent kitchen and breakfast room, separate dining room, separate library and television room with a magnificent drawing room, the apartment is a huge 556 square metres in size. Arguably, its main attraction, however, is its stunning roof terrace. Accessed from the upstairs

PREVIOUS PAGE, TOP AND OPPOSITE / After many years of living in Hong Kong with spectacular views over the South China Sea and beautiful vegetation, Patricia Frost was determined to create a home on the river in the historic part of Bangkok. There are wonderful waterway views here of a different kind, not to mention lush and varied plantings.

LEFT / Aerial view of the temple below. The *ubosot* (ordination hall) appears to be very old, probably pre-dating the founding of Bangkok, although the Chinese style of the *viharn* (prayer hall) suggests that it was built, or rebuilt, in the era of King Rama II.

verandah via a spiral staircase or directly from the master bedroom through sliding doors, it forms a marvellous garden in the sky.

In the past, gardens in Thailand, especially those in metropolitan areas, tended towards the utilitarian, typically featuring culinary and medicinal herbs and plants in pots — and not much more. There may have been the odd fruit tree or small Chinese-style, clipped topiary shrub again in a *jardinière*, but that would have been it. It is only in recent years that the garden has come to be seen potentially as an aesthetic and serene place in which to relax. This 78-square-metre garden, complete with relaxation deck and reflecting pool, is planted with a selection of betel nut palms, spider lilies, ferns, birds of paradise, white bougainvillea, gladioli and sweet jasmine for a verdant jungle effect. Hardscapes in the form of pebbles, stepping stones, low stone walls and outdoor illumination complete the tranquil scene.

It is difficult to tear oneself away from this outdoor eyrie, but contemplation of the apartment and the owners' substantial collection of antique furniture and artefacts makes the move worthwhile. Some modern pieces mix and mingle with Ming-style *zitan* chairs and consoles, while surfaces are home to a variety of collectibles — an antique Thai *bencharong* pot, a Chinese pillow opium box, some Burmese lacquer bowls and more.

Testament to the taste of the owners, Patricia and Richard Frost, a couple who have lived in Asia for many years, the apartment is an elegant reflection of their personalities.

LEFT / A spa-like ambience is created in the master bathroom with an oversized terrazzo tub, textured stone wall and slate floor, not to mention gorgeous garden views. The large ceramic urn is a contemporary Thai piece.

ABOVE / In the master bedroom, a dramatic pink and lime-green palette on the bed sees silk coverings from Chatuchak weekend market, a favourite place to browse for homewares. Behind the bed is an antique Chinese carved wall panel, while knick-knacks on the dressing table include an Art Deco lamp from China, a betel nut container, and a traditional jasmine garland or *phuang malai*.

Urban Tree House

The kidney bean shaped landmass called the Phra Phadaeng peninsula or Bang Krachao (Bangkok's "Green Lung") may not be the obvious place to locate a 12-room boutique inn, but for owner Jirayu (Joey) Talanond it fits the bill perfectly. Describing the 2,000 hectares of semi-wild open space as "Bangkok as it was 200 years ago", he has gone back to his roots.

Literally. For Talanond's escape from the city is built entirely from bamboo and reclaimed wood reinforced with recycled steel and prides itself on its eco credentials. From the floating bamboo arrival pontoon to the 12 "nests" artfully concealed within the trees, as well as a strong environmental ethos, the inn reflects its owner's Green Alphabet: an ambitious A to Z of sustainability principles.

A stands for Air quality control, B for Bamboo structure, C for Carbon free cooking — and so on. It isn't for everyone, Talanond's website cheerfully notes, but for those with an interest in green hospitality and a foray into a less frenetic, more sedate and naturalistic urban experience, the Tree House will surely charm.

The owner worked closely with local architect Nuntagpong Yindeekhun to create an intelligent, modern hideaway hotel that has ample mod-cons but allows nature to take centre stage. The site on the banks of the Chao Phraya River is quite wide on the inland side, but tapers at the riverfront where the central hotel building is located. Housing the public spaces — lobby, restaurant lounge and so on — this structure takes its inspiration from the traditional Thai house that is perched on stilts. This not only impacts lightly on the land and surrounding ecosystem, it also helps with natural ventilation.

Further inland are 12 guest rooms or "nests", artfully arranged amongst the existing trees and

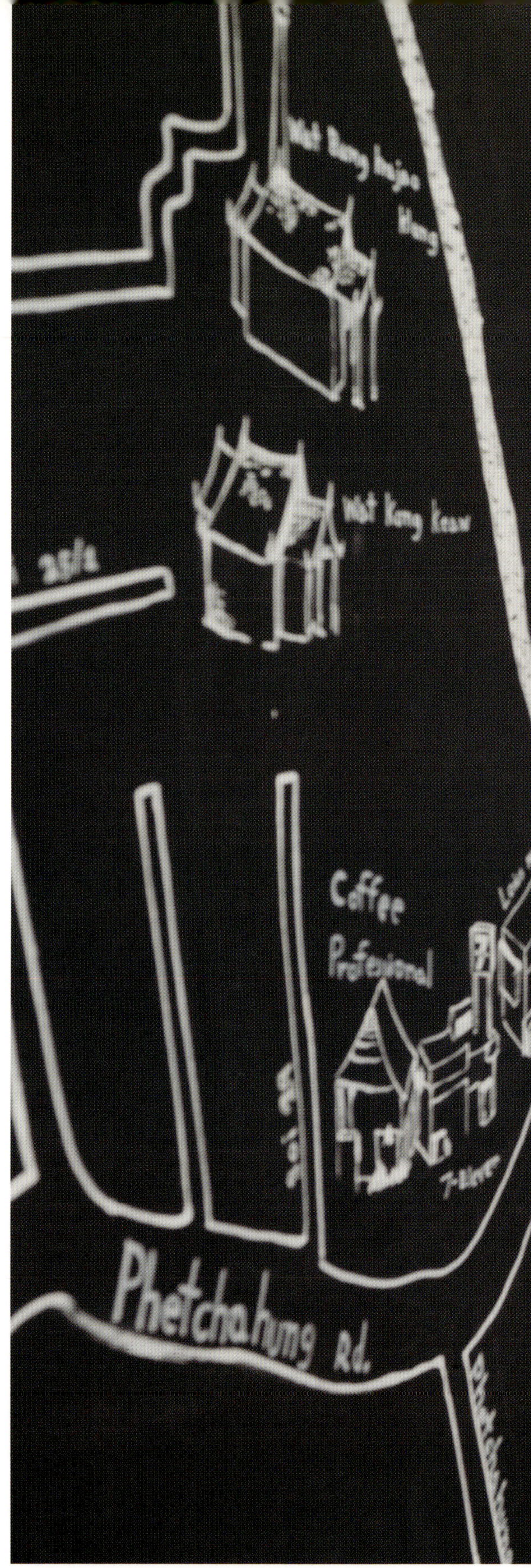

OPPOSITE / Versatile bamboo, used traditionally in Thailand for furniture, kitchen receptacles, fish traps and the like, is used here as both a planter and a grid for plants to climb up.

ABOVE / Messages expounding the owner's environmental ethos in the form of funky signage, helpful graphic maps, inspirational quotes and the like are all incorporated into the design of the hotel.

placed so as to give each accommodation privacy as well as views of jungle and river. An outside bathroom and deck combines with a bedroom that does have air-conditioning. There is good use of timber cladding for insolation and, elsewhere, mirrors are used to make spaces seem larger than they are and to reflect scenery on to the walls of the boxy buildings. There is also a pool that uses aquatic plants to keep the water clean. Similarly, natural micro-organisms are used to treat waste water from the hotel.

Another genuine example of the hotel's commitment to sustainability is its level of communication and consultation with local people. Engagement with the small communities on Phra Phadaeng started well before construction and continued during building — and the dialogue is on-going now the hotel is up and running. Free bicycles and quaint maps are provided to hotel guests who are encouraged to cycle along the peninsula's network of raised cement paths to enjoy the charms of its rural scenery.

Taking its inspiration from Henry David Thoreau's manual for self-sufficiency, *Walden*, the Bangkok Tree House is a rare gem: for every guest that stays, the staff remove one kilogram of rubbish from the Chao Phraya. For every booking, a person sees a real commitment to sustainability in action. In many ways, the guest experience is not dissimilar to life as it must have been in a traditional Thai dwelling in the countryside in the past.

ABOVE / Perched seven metres above ground, the innovative 'View with a Room' provides stars and the sky as a ceiling and trees and forest for walls. The bamboo floors and railing also come free of charge, as does the mosquito net!

OPPOSITE / The three-room 'Family Nest' has a master bedroom, a study that converts into a second bedroom, and a large bathroom — all overlooking the calm scenery of the Chao Praya. The Family Nest also has three green roofs for guests who want to spend more time in the open-air.

THIS PAGE AND OPPOSITE / The final item in the owner's A to Z includes the aim of a zero waste goal. "We are striving to eliminate all types of waste by following our 6 Rs of sustainable living," he says: "Refuse, Refuse, Refuse, then Reduce, Reuse and Recycle." Everywhere you look, these commitments have been translated into reality: The hotel refuses entry to plastic bottles, but house-distilled water in flasks is provided for free; discarded juice cartons insulate walls, the pier is built from used plastic drums and plentiful reclaimed wood is found elsewhere; only the most energy-efficient electricity is used throughout; vegan food is the norm; and rainwater is harvested for plant growing.

This
is made from
otherwise
One man's
GREAT WALL
drift-wood,
have been
TRASH
of Drift-
which
left
is BANGKOK
TREE HOUSE
Wood TRASH
would
to rot.
's treasure!

Baan Suan Sanghob

Baan Suan Sanghob or "Tranquil Garden House" is the home of architect Prabhakorn Vadanyakul and his wife. Situated in the outskirts of the city on a plot of land planted by Khun Prabhakorn's father with seeds collected from around the country, the three-storey house showcases mature trees at every turn. Built predominantly from steel and glass, it may be closed up to take advantage of air-conditioning or parts of the structure may be opened up to invite the outdoors in.

This is entirely how the architect wanted it. He grew up with trees and desired to include nature in his home. At the same time, he is a fan of all things technological and wanted the home to be modern. As such, the house reconciles traditional aspects of Thai dwellings (open-air and among the surrounding trees) with an industrial aesthetic that is more often found in dense urban settings. Having said that, the steel-framed structure never for a minute seems out of place in its jungle situation. Rather, by inviting in light, air, breeze and trees, it appears to fully embrace the surrounding vegetation.

A self-confessed aviation fan (both he and his wife are pilots), Khun Prabhakorn brings his lifelong obsession with the mechanical into the design of the home. Stainless steel tension cables, doors in the shape of those found in planes, a front door handle made from a propeller, steel mesh walkways and exposed pipes are strictly utilitarian. Similarly, aggressively sculptural Mario Botta furniture is used sparingly throughout. Nonetheless, all are softened and humanized by the plethora of vegetation that surrounds the home.

The house took about six months to design and two years to build with the ground-breaking ceremony taking place on the 19th day of the ninth month of the year 1999 at 9am. According to Khun Prabhakorn, steel structures can be slimmer and more lightweight than concrete-heavy ones, so his home always feels airy and spacious. In his own words, he notes: "I wanted to show that nature and technology are not polar issues. In other words, we can choose to live with both, without excluding one from the other."

PREVIOUS PAGE LEFT / Machine technology is everywhere, from steps in the shape of aircraft wing sections, to open ducting and tensioned steel cables supporting everything from a staircase to toilet paper rolls.

PREVIOUS PAGE RIGHT / A massive steel-and-glass end wall on the ground floor rolls away on an overhead curved track to open the house to the terrace and swimming pool.

LEFT TOP / The dining area and open-plan kitchen back onto the living room. All are connected by polished sandstone floors and floor-to-ceiling glass windows which Khun Prabhakorn says act only as space indicators, thereby giving views on to the garden on all sides. The dining table is masculine in style, made from black galvanized steel and glass.

LEFT MIDDLE / The master bedroom features polished cement walls, light wood parquet flooring and factory-style exposed light fittings. The platform bed was custom made.

LEFT BELOW / Plane imagery abounds: an outside bench resembles a plane wing, while the open wood staircase treads were designed to replicate the flaps of an aeroplane's wing.

OPPOSITE / The steel-framed house was designed keeping the site in mind — it fits into a slot between the trees, which press around it. Similarly, the pool seems to melt into the surrounding vegetation.

ABOVE / The industrial aesthetic is evident in all parts of the house. All wirework and plumbing are left exposed, while the house utilizes rolled steel columns and beams, profiled steel formwork for floor plates, solar tinted glass, powder coated aluminium, stainless steel cables in tension and minimal polished wood.

HERITAGE THAI

When one visits a Thai palace, classic Ayutthaya house on stilts or a temple compound, there is no disputing the building's origin and heritage. Such "Thai Style" is unmistakable: there's a plethora of teak; copious use of distinct decorative designs; a tapering shape; a communion with nature. Sometimes all these elements are evident; at others only a few, or even one.

Different homes illustrate this heritage in different ways. Be it a modern residence that doubles up as a treasure trove of antique art and artefacts, an older structure that has withstood the test of time or even a new-build that utilizes recycled wood, it is uniquely Thai in nature. Combining a respect for culture with masterly craftsmanship and age-old motifs, the resulting interiors are usually classic, but often include a modern twist. Many have been updated for contemporary living, but still retain a healthy respect for the past.

ABOVE / Surface decoration of lucky pomegranates and a flying heron on a Chinese wedding cabinet — one of the treasures at Baan Kampun.

OPPOSITE / An intricately carved antique double door with floral and vegetal patterns at the Taylor house in Koh Samui.

Tassana Pra

The name of this vernacular-style house roughly translates as "View of the Buddha" and this is apt, because the slightly elevated home looks out towards Koh Samui's famous Big Buddha statue and temple. Set in the hills above Bangrak, it was conceptualized and built as a dream holiday home.

"Having built Poppies Hotel in Chaweng (with others) using a classic Ayutthaya style for the rooms and restaurant, I always wanted to build a spectacular house for myself in the same style," explains owner John Taylor. "It was built as a home, and to satisfy a long-held desire to combine an authentic, genuine Thai building with up-to-date fittings and fixtures."

As such, the concept and design are old, but the execution fairly new. Five wooden pavilions, set on an elevated concrete floor, combine recycled wood from old houses with newly felled timber. All the wooden columns that support the *salas* are antique as are the floors (teak in the main *sala* and other hardwoods in the bedrooms), while the wall

panels are all constructed from new teak. Some of the floorboards are over a foot wide and sport a wonderful polished patina — the result of many years' use. In keeping with the architectural ethos, the roof is tiled with traditional terracotta tiles made in the Ayutthaya area.

The focus of the home is a huge open-plan living/dining pavilion that is supported by 12 ancient and incredibly tall antique columns. Ventilated by two sets of folding wood-framed glass doors on the east side and three sets on the west side, there is no need for air-conditioning. The west doors open onto a covered balcony, which in turn is open to a further stone-covered terrace. The arrangement is deliberate in order to catch all the cross breezes that blow in both directions. As in traditional homes in Thailand, this pavilion is easily accessed from the other *salas* from each of its four corners.

The house also boasts a verdant landscape and free-form swimming pool with an eco ethos. Taylor is a keen gardener and he designed the pool and garden himself. As the classic Ayutthaya-style house is designed for the central plains where there is plenty of rain and a level flood plain, the Thai house does not have gutters. Koh Samui, on the other hand, experiences low rainfall, so water had to be conserved without the addition of ugly gutters. Taylor explains his *modus operandi*: "I surrounded the house as much as possible with ponds to catch the rainwater. Some upper ponds drain to four main ponds in the garden below, while water in the lowest and largest pond is used for the sprinkler system for the garden. Rainwater falling from the roof onto the stone balcony is also channelled to a storage tank for use in the garden. In addition, there are two huge storage tanks underneath bedrooms 1 and 2 — one for drinking water and one for the garden."

Such forethought is exemplary in an environment where resources are frequently over-stretched. In addition, the luxuriant landscape provides visual drama from many of the home's vantage points.

PREVIOUS PAGE / Set on approximately three *rai* of land, the house's elevated position allows for fabulous views of Big Buddha and the neighbouring island of Koh Phangan in the distance.

OPPOSITE / The magnificent living/dining pavilion also boasts splendid vistas and an interior that combines artworks with a homely feel. Behind the sofa are two wooden *dewa* statues set in niches, while elsewhere celadon, teak, rattan and fabric sourced in Chatuchak market combine to provide a distinctly Thai atmosphere.

RIGHT / Beautifully carved in teak, the main door to the house is painted with a temple guardian design on the inside.

BELOW / With sustainable building a priority, the owner sourced all materials from Thailand, except for some marble from Taiwan and Norwegian slate. Four colours of local sandstone were used in the bathrooms and main balcony, and local slate is on the walls of the lower floor.

ABOVE / The warmth of wood is evident in this small study where a new teak desk and chair looks out over the garden. The carved chest is from Burma, and was sourced at Mae Sot on the Thai/ Burmese border. The carving is actually gilded metal, with cut glass inserts.

ABOVE RIGHT / In the master bedroom (see opposite), a comfy teak armchair sits before a pair of wooden doors, with colours carefully added, hanging on the wall. The cushion on the chair is a northern Thai hill tribe fabric, sewn onto indigo-dyed rough Thai cotton.

ABOVE / The handsome 6m x 4m master bedroom is the only bedroom with an exposed underside of roof and double wood panes with sound insulation between. At the bed's head is a gilded lacquered *hsun-ok* bought in Pagan, Burma, while decorative details include woodcarvings of foliage beneath the windowsills and custom-crafted wall lights in resin. The elegant four-poster originates from Burma, but was modified and restored in Bangkok.

Baan Khampun

Many people in Thailand, especially those in the north east, will be familiar with the *pha kab bua* textile pattern. Translating as "lotus spathe cloth" (the spathe being a bract on the flower that has its own pattern and colour), it has been adopted by Ubon Ratchathani as the province's official cloth. This is apt as the province's name translates as "Royal Land of the Lotus".

What they may not know is that the basic pattern, consisting of two coloured warp threads and a *mudmee* tie-dyed weft thread, was created by Khun Meechai Toe Sujiriya and his mother, Mrs Khampun Srisai. Scions of a wealthy local Sino-Thai family, they have also designed and built an extraordinary mansion which they open once a year to the public as a textile museum.

Consisting of a number of recently built Thai-style wooden structures surrounded by manicured gardens, the Baan Khampun compound adheres strictly to classical Thai construction principles as expounded during the King Rama V period (r 1868–1910). The owners took great pains to recreate an authentic atmosphere, filling the various buildings with antiques and artworks, as well as precious examples of sericulture. North East Thailand, usually called Isaan which means "Northeast", is a multi-ethnic area endowed with a rich textile and costume heritage. The art of weaving has been handed down from generation to generation in these various ethnic groups.

The main focus of the compound is three slightly elevated pavilion-style structures with multi-tiered roofs overlooking a formal lily pond that

PREVIOUS PAGE, LEFT AND RIGHT / One of many Buddha images (left) that are housed in this main pavilion (right) fronting the central lotus pond. This Lotus Pond House, built entirely from hardwood, is used for worship and prayer and for merit-making ceremonies and giving food to the monks. Ancient Chinese ceremonies, in line with the traditions of the homeowner's father, are also performed here.

OPPOSITE TOP / Stairs at the back of the Lotus Pond House lead down to a lawn. Here the pond shows European influences, while the sensuous curve of the balustrade recalls a swirl of water. It culminates in an antique carved stone lion from China.

OPPOSITE BOTTOM / The upper floor of this building housing the bundles of thread used in silk weaving is open on all four sides.

BELOW, LEFT TO RIGHT / A water urn outside the door is usually equipped with a coconut ladle so that feet may be washed before crossing the threshold. A copper candleholder sits atop a lacquer box. A pair of *bai sri* trees, constructed from green banana leaves and flowers, sit on a tray with some gold-and-black lacquer bowls. In Isaan, visitors are often welcomed in a Bai Sri Soo Kwan ceremony where white or coloured strings adorning a *bai sri* are tied around the wrists of honoured guests. An intricate hanging *malai* or garland made from jasmine and crown flowers is ephemeral. Such *malai* are traditionally hung in windows as decoration during weddings or at the ordination ceremony of a male member of the family entering the monkhood.

is surrounded by clipped trees, a form of topiary art known in Thai as *mai dat*. Each is exquisitely decorated and filled to the rafters with precious artworks, both religious and secular. These run the gamut from Buddha images and temple artefacts and furniture to more domestic pieces, such as collections of fans, trinket boxes and the like. There is also plenty of heavy Chinese-style rosewood furniture inlaid with mother-of-pearl, as well as Art Nouveau stenciled wall-coverings and typical Thai-style decorative detailing. Interspersed throughout, of course, is the family's superb collection of textiles.

Once a year, during Ubon Ratchathani's famous Candle Festival, held prior to Buddhist Lent, Baan Khampun opens its doors to the public and provides an insight on its treasures. Sericulture enthusiasts are able to view the queen's attire designed by the Khampun family from the epic movie *King Naresuan* as well as a number of looms, textiles and the like, while others can simply bask in the ambience of an era that no longer exists — or, if it does, is glimpsed only rarely. As the owner notes: "Even though the buildings are new, the atmosphere is very much from the past."

LEFT / Some of the exceptional textiles designed and dyed by the homeowner display various weaving techniques — *mud mee* or tie-dyeing from northeast Thailand; *chok* (supplementary weft) and tapestry or *ko-su* from China. The simultaneous use of such diverse techniques is the hallmark of textiles from Baan Khampun. In addition, there are brocade textiles woven with gold thread combined with intricate tapestry work.

BELOW / Architectural features such as eave brackets or roof finials often sport carved and gilded representations of mythological animals. Left to right: an eave bracket depicting a *hongse* or sacred swan; a *naga* or mythological water serpent doubles up as a door handle; a *naga* head is carved atop an elaborate water faucet.

OPPOSITE TOP / The formal living room has a central cabinet that houses a 700-year-old crystal Buddha image (unseen) dating from the Chiang Saen period.

OPPOSITE BOTTOM / Bedrooms and bathrooms sport both Western and Thai elements: The marble-clad bathroom contains two items of furniture: a Thai low table and a Western-style dresser with mirror; while the bedroom is super comfortable with a teakwood four-poster.

Baan Mier Raap

One of the encouraging features of recent house construction in Thailand has been the emphasis on preservation of nature and conservation of resources. This house in Mae Rim district in Chiang Mai — the holiday home of a prominent artist — is a pertinent case in point.

Set on a 13-*rai* (5-acre) plot of land, the home comprises a main house with an adjoining guest suite and a nearby studio, all overlooking a central lotus pond. Even though the roof tiles and brick

came from a manufacturer in the central province of Ang Thong, all the wood used in construction — for shutters, railings, floors, window and door frames — was bought from the owner of three houses that were damaged by floods a year before construction. Hence, it is all recycled. Also, in keeping with sustainable principles, all flooring, with the exception of the master bedroom, is in polished concrete. Cool underfoot and less pressurized on the environment, it is an attractive, yet functional, surface.

Architect, Ong-Ard Satrabhandhu, has employed two very particular forms in the home: the use of an almost completely continuously encircling verandah at ground floor and a similarly circling balcony at first floor; and the use of multi-hipped roofs. These features are eminently practical, not to mention deeply steeped in the culture of northern Thai architecture. The multi-tiered roof with its extended eaves is inspired by roof forms in Yunnan Province in southwest China; it serves the function (in this case covering both ground and first storey) of protecting and shading from sun and rain. Similarly, the continuous verandahs and balconies encourage cross ventilation (with air cooled by the lotus pond) and give plentiful indoor/outdoor seating options. All are extremely sensible in an area that experiences a harsh tropical climate.

Décor in the house is a mix of international and Thai, combining family heirlooms with locally sourced furniture and furnishings. The living room

is dominated by a huge artwork by Zambian Thai artist Sakarin Krue-on, most well-known for works whereby he takes traditional elements and places them into modern media such as installations, murals and videos. This oversized portrait does not have any connection to the home owner's family, but is clearly taken from a former formal portrait. Juxtaposed with black-and-white family photos on a low console, it makes a striking statement.

Bedrooms and bathrooms, in both the guest wing and the upper floor, are a similar combination of the traditional and the modern. White-painted bedroom furniture, slightly distressed for a contemporary feel, works well with dark wood and carefully selected artworks. The owner sourced most of the furniture from Mae Sot, a district that borders Burma. Most of the pieces had to be repaired, refinished or restored, which doubtless contributes to their fresh appeal.

Overall, the home has a relaxed, yet elegant feel, that is contemplative in mood. The colour palette is muted, which brings attention to the top quality finishing and detailing. High ceilings, multiple doors, fanlights and windows, and a series of indoor/outdoor spaces encourage interaction between the lush natural setting and the indoors. At holiday time, it is the ideal place for all the family to gather together.

PREVIOUS PAGE / Completed in 2007, the main house, guest suite and studio are situated in a country setting around a lotus pond that was enlarged.

OPPOSITE / In the comfy living room scatter rugs cover a floor of polished concrete inserted with wooden strips. They add colour and texture to the sofa sets and cushions sourced from Jim Thompson. Cushions covered with *toile de Jouy* calico reflecting a pastoral idyll are in keeping with the natural setting of the home. The two glass platters on the coffee table were a house warming gift.

BELOW / A round table that belonged to the owner's great grandmother has been refinished with metallic motorcycle paint for an on-trend look.

RIGHT / Located underneath the stairs leading to the master bedroom is a Zen-style floating sculpture by Thai artist, Sutee Kunavichayanont.

OPPOSITE TOP / The master bedroom is a symphony of white and wood, with furniture in distressed white sourced from a shop in Chiang Mai called L'Aredo. Colour is focused on a few choice pieces: the red and gold painting above the shelving unit painted by the owner; rugs on either side of the bed — they are Bajastar kilim from Iran, sourced from a dealer in Bangkok; and a red-lacquered altar table at the bed head (partially seen) that was sourced in Mae Sot.

OPPOSITE BOTTOM / Designed for the owner's parents, a twin-bedded room is partially seen through this door. The painting is by the owner, while the black wooden wardrobe in the corridor is an old piece from Mae Sot which is used to store the house's linen collection.

ABOVE / The master bathroom sports a monochrome painting by a Chinese artist from Shanghai. The door next to the tub opens out to the first-floor balcony.

Thai Art in a Modern Home

The unassuming face of this 1980s' house in Lat Phrao in Bangkok doesn't look out of the ordinary from the street. However, once one steps over the threshold one enters a different world — a home chock-a-block with an astonishing collection of Thai religious and secular art and artefacts. It is amazing how looks can deceive.

The Visetsiri house is the home of cat lovers: a husband and wife who enjoy collecting and their daughter. Comprising two floors which open out to a verdant garden and swimming pool, its main focus is the large open-plan living and dining room on the ground floor.

When one enters this room, it is difficult to know where to look first. Every surface seems to be covered with some extraordinary item. The main seating appears to be on two large low-level antique *tangs* that separate the dining table from the living area, although there is further Thai-style seating on low-level triangular cushions set on a dark red antique Indian rug. Pride of place is given to a large painting by an art student that depicts Thailand's verdant vegetation, while a gold sculpture of a curtain flanked by two enormous Thai elephant tusks acts as a backdrop to a flamboyant *hongse* or mythical bird statue. In front of the painting is another golden statue, this time of a deer, while elsewhere a number of clocks keep perfect time: a German grandfather clock; two English London wall clocks and; in the dining room, a French clock with bronze sculpture.

The dining area is no less spectacular with an antique glass-topped table in Western style surrounded by glass-paned scripture cabinets housing some superb collections: an extremely rare mother-of-pearl inlay monk alms' bowl cover made for the coronation of King Chulalongkorn in 1873; some Thai-style crystal, gold and nielloware; as well as a vast collection of Chinese blue-and-white ceramics dating from the Qing Dynasty. Two beautiful

PREVIOUS PAGE LEFT / Given by King Chulalongkorn to some senior monks attending his coronation ceremony, this alms' bowl cover is very rare. Carved from mother-of-pearl, the top section depicts a coronet on a double-tiered tray which is the monogram of the king. It is flanked by two multi-tiered parasols, all of which are carried by a three-headed elephant.

PREVIOUS PAGE RIGHT / In traditional Thai homes, seating was always on the floor. Although the living room is superlatively furnished and decorated, the time-honoured Thai custom of sitting on floor-level cushions is maintained.

ABOVE / A mix of Western and Eastern elements, the dining room makes a flamboyant statement in sumptuous gold and red. The Western-style table is juxtaposed by antique daybeds covered with contemporary silk textiles sourced from a shop called Kompatra in Bangkok, while an assortment of rare antiques is housed in two scripture cabinets.

OPPOSITE / Even though the *sangkhet* takes pride of place in this gorgeous Shrine Hall, there are some other gems to note also. The low pulpit and the Buddha image stand are from the Bangkok Period, while the thin cabinet is a candle stand used in the *ubosot* or ordination hall of a temple. In the foreground is a contemporary lantern in Moroccan style bought from the Chatuchak weekend market in Bangkok.

gold-painted cabinets from the Fifth Reign set at an angle to each other flank a large window with views of the garden. Between them and set atop a pedestal is a large statue of a Thai *hongse* — with wings and tail fluttering it looks as if it has just flown in through the window and perched for a short rest.

As if this were not enough already, the pride of the owners' collection may well be their huge Buddhist pulpit that is housed in a room adjacent to the swimming pool. Bought at auction a few years ago, it used to belong to Doris Duke, the American heiress, philanthropist and art collector. Called a *sanghet* in Thai, it was designed to house four monks who used it for chanting. Consisting of a horizontal wide seat raised on a platform and covered with a tiered roof, it is intricately carved and decorated and now houses a statue of the Buddha. Duke displayed it in her Thai Village re-creation in Hawaii, a project that she set up to educate the American public about Southeast Asian art and culture. It is entirely fitting that this dedicated family of collectors has facilitated the *sanghet*'s return to its native soil.

TOP / A special set of containers used for a water blessing set on a nielloware tray dates from the mid 19th-century Bangkok Period. Used at weddings or other auspicious ceremonies, the golden conch shell contains consecrated water, while the other two nielloware containers with gold tops contain powders and wax.

OPPOSITE BELOW / Another rare gem in the Visetsiri collection is a courtly cosmetics set that includes a centrepiece in the form of a green crystal perfume container with gold top. The seven nielloware containers are for herbal cosmetics for the face and body.

ABOVE / The lush garden, overgrown with a slightly chaotic assortment of ferns, shrubs and trees, is a haven of quiet and green. Adjacent a bench and table painted a lovely aqua colour are some reproduction stone carvings bought from the weekend market.

Reworking Tradition

Even though this is a 21st-century build, we include this seaside house in our heritage chapter because it was conceived as a modern version of the archetypal Thai house of the central plains. The traditional form of such structures included a number of units, set on stilts, and linked by platforms and terraces. The intention in this house was to rework these traditional techniques in a

modern idiom, particularly those developed to keep living spaces cool, shaded and connected to the green exterior.

Situated near the resort town of Pattaya on Thailand's eastern seaboard, the site for this holiday home on a gentle slope of a low range of hills was carefully chosen for its wide view over the coast. Architects 49, the architectural firm, decided on a two-storey structure that used wood extensively, but also included steel beams and local stone for added interest. The form, however, resembles that of a traditional Thai house, with the upper floor and roof projecting out over the lower floor. Even though modern tiles instead of traditional wood or thatch were used for the roof, they still have the same function of sheltering the verandahs with a deep overhang. Similarly, there is a seamless flow from indoor to outdoor spaces and every room within the home invites views of pool, sea or garden.

The roof, in particular, was carefully thought-through. The distinctive, steeply pitched Thai roof form works on small domestic units and large halls or palaces, but would not have worked in this large two-storey home. Nor was its heat-extraction

PREVIOUS PAGE / Views of the house, pool and *sala*. For the most part wood dominates — in the post-and-beam structure, for shutters and many of the walls, and for the extensive decking that connects the buildings around the pool.

OPPOSITE TOP / The woodwork is particularly fine: in addition to sliding French windows, there are also louvred sliding shutters for additional security.

OPPOSITE BELOW / The dining room has a carefully framed view of the lush vegetation outside. Above the sideboard on right is a gold leaf on wood Tree of Life painting.

RIGHT / A projection of the roof all around, supported by eave brackets, is an important element in construction in the Thai house. It is essential for comfort in the tropical climate. Here we see some close-ups of the joinery — how the slim eaves project up from the floor at an angle to join the underside of the roof.

function necessary, as shutters and sliding glass panels were designed to open both floors on three sides for ventilation. The architects decided, therefore, to create less pitch with two tiers, but still keep the deep overhang. This called for a contemporary version of the classical Thai eave bracket.

In traditional structures, the eave bracket is often a work of art in itself. Palaces and temples in central Thailand often use the *kanok* vine motif, whereas in the north, there are two types: a triangular piece of wood called a *hu chang* (elephant ear) or a longer rectangular version. Both are usually carved with the design of a specific figure, often a *naga* or another mythological animal. Rows of such eave brackets, sometimes painted in bright colours, are one of Thailand's architectural treasures.

Throughout this home, the eave brackets are slim and simple, rising from floor level to the roof. Beautifully planed, they project out from the base of the verandah, through the balustrade, to the outer lip of the roof. As such, they have a character all their own.

Chakrabongse House and Villas

Originally the residence of Prince Chakrabongse of Phitsanulok and his wife Ekaterina Ivanova Desnitskaya, also known as Katya, Chakrabongse House is now the residence of their grand-daughter Mom Rajawongse Narisa Chakrabongse, an eminent publisher and environmentalist. Set on a one-acre site at Ta Tien in Bangkok directly opposite Wat Arun or the Temple of the Dawn, it was originally envisaged as a simple retreat for boating excursions on the river and for pre- or post-attendance at state ceremonies in the nearby Grand Palace.

Designed by an Italian architect Mario Tamagno, one of several Italian architects in Bangkok at the time, the villa dates from 1908. Built along classical lines, it is a curious East/West mix. A central tower with a "widow's walk", a standard decorative feature of Italianate architecture, is its most obvious idiosyncrasy, but it also features verandahs and balconies with wide overhangs that are clearly orientated towards living in the tropics. Protecting from both burning sun and tropical downpours, they provide for cool seating areas, at upper- and ground-storey levels.

The interior is also cool with carved air vents above doors inviting cross ventilation and high ceilings ensuring good air flow. Furnished with dark wood paneling, polished marble or wooden floors,

some choice antiques along with a treasure trove of family portraits, photos and mementoes, it is both home and historical repository.

The garden is no less alluring, featuring lush plantings, a garden pavilion originally built by a Russian carpenter for the family home at Hua Hin, a formal reflecting pool with a glass sculpture by Danny Lane, as well as a swimming pool. It now houses one of Bangkok's best kept secrets — a boutique-style hostelry with four suites housed in some teak cottages by the river and an annex containing a further three rooms for those travelling on more of a budget.

These accommodations are almost a microcosm of the difficult-to-categorise Thai Style, as they contain influences from most parts of Asia in their décor. The Thai House, overlooking the pond, is situated in a beautifully re-constructed wooden building from

OPPOSITE / View of the house from the leafy garden that is landscaped with a number of striking water features.

ABOVE / This superb piece from the American sculptor Danny Lane is sited in a small pool in the garden. Known mainly for his works in glass, the artist is based in London.

Ayutthaya that was dismantled, transported and reassembled piece by piece on site. The River View Suite, as its name suggests, keeps visitors occupied on its gorgeous verandah by the activity on the Chao Phraya; below it is the Garden Suite. For a touch of Oriental opulence, guests may opt for the Chinese Suite, a two-bedroom house with an enclosed living room and spacious verandah, decorated with antique lacquered cabinets, carved screens and a sumptuous Chinese four-poster bed in the master bedroom. The annex with three smaller double rooms is still characterful and decorated with a smattering of exotica — old Moroccan doors, Indian beds and the like, brought back by the owner from foreign travels.

Dining is another highlight at Chakrabongse Villas: in the evening Thai delicacies concocted for the court are dished up and served at simple riverside tables overlooking the beautifully illuminated Wat Arun. With friendly service and intriguing flavours, a dinner here is wonderfully atmospheric, evoking as it does an aura from an earlier era in history.

OPPOSITE / The beautifully appointed dining room in Chakrabongse House is set up for a formal dinner. The portrait at the head of the table is of King Chulalongkorn, while the porcelain on the sideboard is *bencharong*, Chinese-made five colour ware. These wares were very collectible in the late 19th and early 20th centuries.

RIGHT TOP / The conservatory was added by the owner to create a relaxed dining and sitting area linking the garden and the interior.

RIGHT BOTTOM / The entrance hall is panelled in teak and has a mix of antiques and modern art with a light sculpture by Berlin-based South Korean artist Haegue Yang.

OPPOSITE TOP / An attractive feature of Chakrabongse Villas is the golden teak floors, panelling and doors.

OPPOSITE BOTTOM / The drawing room has family portraits as well as a collection of mother-of-pearl antiques.

RIGHT TOP / The former study of HRH Prince Chula Chakrabongse, the owner's father, is reflective and quiet. This was where he wrote many of his best-selling books on Thai history.

RIGHT BOTTOM / The upper landing showing the teak staircase.

OPPOSITE / Ideally situated on the river and close to all the royal attractions in Bangkok, Chakrabongse Villas is a leafy oasis of calm in the middle of town. Here we see two sumptuous bedrooms that offer guests both comfort and atmosphere. Furnished in the rich hues of burnished teak and earth-toned silks, they evoke an earlier era. Owner, M R Narisa Chakrabongse, explains the *raison d'etre* for the hotel: "Having grown up in the main house at Chakrabongse Villas and watched the sun set over Wat Arun, I really wanted to share my love for my home with special guests."

The top bedroom in the Thai House suite features bamboo lights fashioned by a local designer and an elegant four-poster bed with drapes. The photo below is the River View suite which has a bedroom, sitting room and study all contained in a teak, Thai-style house.

ABOVE / The wonderfully romantic nighttime view over the Chao Phraya river to Wat Arun from Chakrabongse Villas is one of the highlights of a visit to this characterful inn. Diners can enjoy a daily changing menu of classic royal Thai dishes.

Riverside Retreat

When King Chulalongkorn signed an 1883 treaty securing British access to the Siamese Kingdom's vast northern teak forests, a corresponding decree obliged foreign timber merchants in Chiang Mai to live on the east bank of the Ping River — the opposite side from the Thais. They settled near Wat Gatekaram, a venerable wooden temple that lent its name to the surrounding area. A scattering of these private homes built from teakwood with ample cross ventilation and slatted shutters still remains.

These buildings, along with some local rural homes mainly constructed from wood, provided the inspiration for this tranquil compound. Housing an excellent restaurant as well as a home, the project was the brainchild of renowned owner and architect Ajarn (Professor) Chulathat Kitibutr. Set on a serene curve in the river, each of its individual structures has fabulous mountain views. The location was the clincher as far as the architect owner was concerned. "Usually the river goes straight all the time," he notes, "so finding a piece of land on a curve was paramount."

Consisting of a series of buildings with multi-level porches and verandahs, a number of pavilions and gazebos and a riverside boat docking *sala* set in quiet, leafy landscaping, the charm of the compound lies in its pastoral setting and its elegant, yet rustic, architecture. The entire project took one and a half years to complete. Mostly using locally available materials such as teak, toddy-palm trunks, bamboo and local terracotta tiles, Ajarn Chulathat imported from a nearby village a team of craftsmen, well practised in woodworking, to help with the construction work.

Certainly the view, especially at sunset when the sun's colours are reflected in the sluggish Ping River waters and the mountains are etched against the sky, is a potent draw. Another attraction is the much lauded food at the Baan Suan restaurant. But, for many, it is the multiple pavilion-style buildings overlooking the river that have the greatest appeal. For a piece of old Lanna and Burmese style, the serenity of the Thai countryside is hard to beat.

OPPOSITE / Sporting a centre pinnacle, as in Lanna architecture, this locally made lounger is a good example of Chiang Mai craftsmanship.

RIGHT / The main dining room can be opened to the elements so that diners have all-encompassing views of the Ping River. Furniture is from Chiang Mai: rattan and wood chairs; sturdy teak tables; and a multi-tiered chandelier. A boat dcking jetty and *sala* can be seen through the restaurant in the background.

OPPOSITE TOP / The two-tiered and hipped roof of this pavilion is typical of residential architecture in the Chiang Mai area. It offers plentiful shade and protection from rain, and also adds stability to the overall structure.

OPPOSITE BOTTOM / Raised high on stilts, this tree-house style structure would have been used as a rice granary in the past. The expansive area beneath formed an undercroft where tools, looms and even animals would have been kept.

THIS PAGE / The dark tones of shiny teakwood contrast with a cool white palette in the furnishings and fabrics in this bedroom wing. A seating area with TV and DVD player is separated from the mosquito net-clad bed by a sturdy rattan screen, while the antechamber features a standing Buddha image flanked by a pair of over-sized candlesticks.

ACKNOWLEDGEMENTS

The photographer and author would like to thank the following homeowners, hotel groups and other personnel for all their help during the production of this book:

Mom Rajawongse Narisa Chakrabongse

Mom Rajawongse Charuvan Rangsit

Khun Ad Boonkrong Indhusophon

Visetsiri family

Khun Jakkai Siributr

John Taylor

Godelieva Aerts and Robert Powell

Khun Prabhakorn Vadanyakul

Patricia and Richard Frost

Michelle Han

Khun Montri Virojnvechapant

Ajarn Chulathat Kitibutr

Cindi Novkov

Khun Meechai Toe Sujiriya and Mrs Khampun Srisai of Baan Khampun

Khun Jirayu Talanond of the Bangkok Tree House

Gabriela Henrichwark and Ming Tan of COMO Hotels and Resorts

Jaime Quek of Design Hotels™

Khun Francis Gan from The Library, Koh Samui

Khun Ratree Poowichai of Veranda Resort and Spa

Khun Chompoopann Wajitdon of SALA Hospitality Group

Detlef Dirksen, Jan Bisping, Khun Kanyapha Kitjapirak and Shelly Poplak of Tamarind Springs

Staff at The Treasure, Koh Madsum

Staff at The Rachamankha

Staff at The Siam Hotel, Bangkok

Staff at Sofitel So, Bangkok

Staff at lub.D hostel, Bangkok

Staff at the Ping Nakara hotel, Chiang Mai

Staff at Sedhapura by Tohsang

Khun Duangrit Bunnag and Khun Siriporn of DBALP

Dr Manas Soongprasit

Khun Pahtt Viravaidya

Neyla Freeman

Khun Paisarn Piemmettawat

PHOTO CREDITS

All photography is by Michael Freeman with the exception of the images listed below:

Pages 50–59: courtesy of DBALP
Pages 68, 70 bottom, 71 bottom, 73 top, 74, back cover: courtesy of Gillian Beal
Pages 69, 70 top, 71 top, 72, 73 bottom, 75: courtesy of COMO Hotels and Resorts
Pages 86–87: courtesy of Anantara, Chiang Mai
Pages 102–107: courtesy of The Library, Koh Samui
Page 109 top: courtesy of SALA Hospitality Group
Pages 126 top, 128–131: courtesy of Tamarind Springs, Samui
Pages 183, 184, 185 bottom: courtesy of Paisarn Piemmettawat, River Books, Bangkok

HOTEL AND RESORT LISTINGS

www.designhotels.com
www.bangkoktreehouse.com
www.comohotels.com/pointyamu/
http://chiang-mai.anantara.com/
www.rachamankha.com
http://salaresorts.com/khaoyai/
www.silom.lubd.com
www.sofitel-so-bangkok.com
www.tamarindsprings.com
http://thelibrary.co.th/
www.thesiamhotel.com
www.tohsang.com/sedhapura/eng/about.htm
www.thetreasureresort.com/kohmadsum
http://www.verandaresortandspa.com/verandachiangmai